Living
With
Sorrow

Living
With
Sorrow

by
DENNIS J. GEANEY

THOMAS
MORE
PRESS

ISBN: 0-88347-074-8

Contents

Introduction

This book is concerned with the experience of loss and how people come to terms with, or live with, the sorrow and grief it evokes. One view of loss is to see it as a tragedy that should never have occurred. Another is to see loss as simply a part of life. The first view sees life idealistically, what in fantasy it could be, a limitless potential for joy or happiness. This view is exciting but it could be suicidal when life does not deliver the goodies our fantasies seem to promise. The second view sees life as a river with its curves, its ups and downs, ins and outs. It sees life in its totality rather than its parts. This roller coaster view allows for the heights of ecstasy and the depths of depression. Every turn in life is not for better or worse but simply a twist in the course that will reverse itself if we do not panic. It is a spiral view or the crooked line with which God writes straight.

One would think grief would come easily, naturally and at once to one who has read all the journals on grief and attended the lectures of the professionals. But when the time actually comes, we find that reading about grief or discussing the subject does not automatically release the bottled-up feelings that make good grief possible. The body or one's emotions have their own approach to life of which the mind might be unaware.

The frustration which occurs goes something like this: Body says to the mind of the one who wants to release feelings and get on with life: "You know the techniques. You can set the stage, pull back the curtains and say to the emotions, 'Do your thing.'" Emotion, now that the poor intellectually driven person is a captive, replies with sarcasm: "I am in control of the grieving process, not your professors or your mind. I will pull the levers when I am ready. This will not happen until you give up your schizophrenic approach to life, not until your emotions and reason wed and live a holistic life." We cannot commandeer the grief process. All you and I can do is sit by with our frustrations compounded unless we have our head and heart together and can flow with life. .

Learning about grief through reading or discussion is not grieving. Grief, like grace, God or Spirit, chooses its time and place. It refuses to bow to a computerized world. "There is an appointed time for everything. . . . A time to weep, and a time to laugh, a time to mourn, and a time to dance. . . ." Since the appointed time is not ours to choose, one feels embarrassed, powerless, and frustrated when someone tells us we should cry, be angry, feel our guilt or express our anxiety. These emotions are going to do their act when they are ready, if we let them.

We cannot attribute grieving or mourning to an antiseptic, programmed, intellectual decision. It matters not whether our philosophy holds God to be the mighty, external manipulator of our lives or the source of the life which courses through natural events. Grief is beyond our control.

In the face of our loss and our powerlessness to express our feelings, we can do nothing but live with our sorrow. In this sense *Living With Sorrow* is a healthy stance toward life. It is what all great civilizations taught its people, that is, to enter the pain of the event, to stand naked before the mystery of God, to listen to the pain and not run to the drug or liquor store to escape from the pain of living. To eliminate sorrow or grieving is to cut away the deepest source of what makes us human. Without grieving there can be no joy, no creativeness, no sensitivity to the wails of suffering people everywhere. The person who does not grieve blocks off the possibility of a deep, growing, and abiding love. The person who is unwilling to enter the pain of loss is making a death wish.

How long does one have to live in sorrow? Since the termination of the sorrow is not in our hands, we cannot predict. There is no answer. It may be days, weeks, months or years. It may be a life of sorrow;

never a day spent without some twinge of pain. Sorrow then is something we live with. Our only choice is what we do with it. We have the choice of using it constructively as we do when we fully acknowledge our pain and learn from it that nothing material can heal us and make us whole. Only in God do we experience surcease. Or we can choose to bury our sorrow, denying it and thereby thwarting the healing process. Briefly, the choice is to deepen our humanity by entering our sorrow or to develop a thicker shell around our personhood so that we will never feel our own pain or another's. The choice is to let the event speak to us and give meaning to it so that we can make it a part of our lives or keep compulsively busy so that no meaning can possibly emerge.

Entering the pain of sorrow is like driving on an icy street. The temptation is to steer away from it, which means disaster. The way of avoiding disaster and keeping the car straight is to turn the wheels in the direction you do not want the car to go. It is to act against your instincts. It can be a traumatic experience for a beginner. Entering the pain of sorrow is the feeling of high risk, to let our defenses crumble and seemingly court disaster.

Sorrow pushes us to dredge up our faith resources. For many "born" Catholics faith is something imposed from an outside source. We are told how to interpret our experiences, what the event *should* mean. A Catholic home, school, and culture can reinforce these "shoulds" to the point that we have never had to ask ourselves whether what we are told we should experience is indeed congruent with our lived experience. What we are told to believe and we say we believe may not, when the chips are down, be what indeed we *do* believe.

It may be comforting for Catholics to know that they have a whole faith system that goes from the cradle to the grave. This is comforting until we come to a major crisis like a death of a significant person which blows the cover on all the unexamined statements we have made part of our religious baggage. The so-called religious man or woman suddenly becomes an atheist. The God of statements like "God loves" or "God saves" is not present in the clutches. Then begins the long process of building an internal faith. This means that we keep looking at the experience we are involved in until meanings or understandings slowly emerge. Our personal history, our remembrances of how we managed previous crises, becomes our greatest tool. In these moments we may experience the Spirit. It is the fertile ground for the seed of divine life to take root and flower into a lived or experienced faith. Sorrow or grief when willingly entered in a prayerful or reflective style of life opens to us the gift of a deeper level of faith.

Another name for sorrow or grieving is mourning. It is a good old Anglo-Saxon word that has borne the fate of billions of people over thousands of years. In my childhood there were outward, ritual signs of mourning that were carry-overs from European cultures. The crepe on the door of the deceased; the black armbands on men and the black dresses worn by the women. The purple bunting on the public buildings when there was the death of a public official is a relic of that era—that era which instinctually knew more about grief, sorrow and mourning than our more intellectual, sophisticated, antiseptic age. Their familial and public mourning rituals were interpreted as respect for the deceased, but in reality they were ways society offered to help the bereaved listen to their own feelings and express them.

Somehow our culture has dropped these customs and offers no public ways to focus grief. Even our revised Catholic liturgy in its effort to emphasize the message of hope seems too quick to pass over the need for grief. The old *Dies irae,* the black vestments and the heavy mood bespoke of our feelings of loss, of loneliness, and of frustration at having a part of us cut away. It did not try to put death in a celebrative, joyful context when we were still grieving. The word mournful has slipped from our vocabulary. It seems as though mourning were something we should rise above quickly and get on with life through the power of positive thinking, Darvon, alcohol, marijuana or a year's subscription to *Psychology Today*. In *The Death of a Salesman*, Willy Lohman's wife said at her husband's death, "Attention must be paid." He filled a place in her life, in the family and in society, however inadequately. He was a victim of our American dream. Even his destruction needs to be mourned.

We might well question our new liturgy for the deceased and ask ourselves if we are too much in a hurry to pass over the painfulness of grieving and substituting the resurrection before the mourning is finished. There can be no rising from sorrow until we have emotionally experienced the death. Our Old Testament literature was a far cry from the American scene which displays man as too efficient, too enlightened to submit to sorrow.

Sorrow can turn into joy, agony into ecstasy, abandonment by God into trust in God, but not until we have walked in the valley of darkness. It is not until then do we feel the power of the resurrection, the touch of God's hand. Then we can appreciate the range of feelings, from despair to hope which we find in Psalm 42. The psalmist prays:

> My tears are my food day and night,
> as they say to me day after day,
> "Where is your God?"

Why are you so downcast, o my soul?
Why do you sigh within me?

Within me my soul is downcast

Deep calls unto deep
in the roar of your cataracts;
All your breakers and your billows
pass over me.

By day the Lord bestows his grace,
and at night I have his song,
a prayer to my living God.

I sing to God, my rock:
   "Why do you forget me?"
Why must I go about in mourning,
with the enemy oppressing me?

It is only after those in sorrow let themselves be immersed in these feelings of self-pity and abandonment can the psalmist end with his plea for hope:

Hope in God! For I shall again be thanking him,
   in the presence of my savior and my God.

The plan for *Living with Sorrow* is first to identify the catastrophic losses in life; second, to seek an understanding of the grief process; third, spell out some of the psychological dynamics involved in the

healing process; last, to look at our spiritual resources to discover how God is at work and available to us as we move through this sorrow.

This book is not meant to take away our sorrow
but to help us understand it, live with it, and hopefully to cherish it as an unasked for gift of God.

CHAPTER ONE
Identifying Our Losses

Losses are daily occurrences. We are not dealing
here with race track losses, painful loss of a pet, or
the loss of weight which can be joyfully celebrated at
the next weight-watchers weigh-in. There are small
losses in the category of the anxiety of waiting for a
friend who does not arrive for a party or the anger at
the absence of a spouse who pledged punctuality. If
we overly react to one of these small losses, it might
be triggering grief over a larger past loss which we
have not identified. In this book, however, we are
concerned only with the larger losses: the death of a
spouse, family break-up through divorce, a loss of
job, a move, an incurable illness—the losses that
disrupt the flow of life for any healthy person and
become the source of deep sorrow for all mankind.
But we also want to take note of the social, the less
specific losses, represented by neighborhoods in
transition, the loss of civic institutions and the ero-
sion of national and religious symbols which held
life together in a larger web than the nuclear family
and with more person communication than the elec-
tronic media devices.

We offer in this chapter some vignettes of people
in grief to flesh out the wide spectrum of losses in

human life and to sensitize us to the movements in our own lives that bring us to grief.

* * *

After a grueling school year of teaching, I travel to a friend's parish rectory in a distant city for some rest and relaxation. I feel that I am far removed from the hub of action, but not for long. My host takes me the next day to accompany him on a pastoral visit. John Jackson is not in drydock for repairs. He is waiting for the end. He was a builder. A hard bargainer with the union and the city, a man of unflinching honesty and integrity. His wife lovingly glances at him now and again as he holds court in the living room with these two men of the cloth from a centrally located chair which has been shaped from the many months of sitting in it. He is wearing a bathrobe over pajamas and blue socks. Most of the rest of his life will be spent in this bathrobe and this chair.

With an ironclad will he put on a suit this Saturday and walked down the aisle with his only daughter. He will do it no matter what the pain or how it might shorten his life. Then he will go back to the pajamas or a hospital gown until he dies.

The inner power of the man is overwhelming. He knows what life is about. He is a hard-bitten realist and tells how he insisted that the doctors put the facts on the line. He can face the worst. The conversation is light. It touches on the foibles of the personalities he encountered in his life. He speaks, not with disdain, but with sympathetic understanding of their human weaknesses. He can still laugh at their foibles as he approaches death. He is very concerned about a poor girl in the parish who has no good clothes for summer camp. He has asked with feeling that the best be bought for her—no hand-me-downs. I was intrigued. Where did this man's courage come from that he could talk about his own death as something ordinary and not lose his sense of humor as life ebbed away? What source does he tap to empower him to face death with good cheer?

* * *

The next stop was a plush suburb. Joe Jones was in his garden clad in shorts, weeding cabbages. As he saw us approach he brought his six-foot four-inch, tan, 60-year old body to the outdoor swimming pool where we could chat away the rest of the day. His history, as the hours of conversation passed, began to come together. He interrupted at one point to give me a baseball cap to protect my bald head from the noon-day sun. He was a cop whose liberal, humane, intellectually honest approach to law enforcement brought him many promotions and finally an early "forced" retirement. He was the voice of conscience that disturbed peers who preferred that he be put on a "retiree-pedestal" away from the seats of power at headquarters.

Underneath he was hurt, but on the surface he only talked about how good life had been to him. He did not want to talk about his new status as a retiree beyond the care of cabbages and what he learned about barbecuing. I was secretly wondering how he really felt about his separation from the work he loved. As I toured the home before leaving, I noticed a priedieu in his bedroom. It was a symbol of the inner strength that came to him from prayer. It still did not tell me how he dealt with his feeling of loss, except that a rich inner life with God was part of it.

* * *

The scene is my favorite Italian restaurant. Veal parmagiana and veal scallopini are the delicious dishes that come from the personal touch of Alfredo, the co-owner and chef. The well-appointed restaurant, in Italian decor, has few patrons these days. Alfredo has time to leave the kitchen and chat with me. It is no longer open for lunches where local businessmen had double martinis to get through the afternoon and dull their taste for his excellent cooking. The reason for an empty house is called neighborhood change, a social disease comparable to physical killers like cancer.

Alfredo talked about the way things were and the way they are. He would like to sell the establishment for the $110,000 mortgage and let go down the drain the twenty years of profits and life blood he poured into the business. He is tempted to sacrifice the satisfaction he gained from preparing food with great care and artistry. He thinks of severing the ties with the many folks whose appreciation for his culinary art brought them in close contact with him over and over again. He has been offered $90,000. To accept the offer he would have to borrow $20,000 just to give the key to another. Someday he may put a padlock on the door and walk away from his palace as he would from a cemetery after burying a loved one. How would he grieve?

Within the same week I called a friend of Lithuanian origin whom I had not talked to in a few years, for a simple piece of information. It developed into a sharing session. He had finally paid for the three-flat in which he had been living. At last he owned income producing property in a time of economic insecurity. That was the good news. The bad news was that Arabs, Mexicans, and blacks were replacing the Irish, Polish and Lithuanian neighbors who, before the arrivals of the newcomers, gave it the lowest crime rate in the city. It is a neighborhood with good transportation, schools, stores and all the facilities one needs for a self-contained neighborhood that has a sense of pride in its family, religion and work values. It is this kind of neighborhood which makes a city, rather than the gaudy downtown attractions. When the neighborhoods go, the city is dead or is feeling the death pangs.

How long before the neighborhood world he finds so satisfying will change to the point he will feel forced to move to a foreign suburb at an age when he cannot easily put roots down again, as he and his wife did twenty years ago? I was surprised at this man of few words talking at such length and with such feelings.

Like the restaurant owner, he was feeling guilty for his feelings. Like the restaurant owner, he explained he was not a bigot. He was not against the blacks. He had spent a decade working for peaceful integration. In his city it was a common feeling, in neighborhood after neighborhood, that an inevitable flight to a suburb would climax years of patient endurance. He talked about his childhood neighborhood which was still intact despite the perceived threat of racial change. He was anticipating the loss of the social context of his family life which was fleshed out in buildings, institutions, and customs that have meaning in his life.

The satisfactions that made life worthwhile were slipping through his hands. He had made his contribution as a generous Christian. He had supported community meetings that tried to arrest complete cultural change. Everything of import in

21

his life was slipping through his fingers like sand. He felt powerless and sad. The Italian restaurant owner and the Lithuanian homeowner, both children of immigrants, were seeing their ethnic neighborhoods, a rich part of America, die. I had no advice for my friends who would pack their belongings and leave behind the scenes of childhood and adult contentment. I was simply a sympathetic listener.

While the transition of a familiar neighborhood, which represents one's cultural heritage, brings personal loss, grief, and sorrow to one's life, such a thing as the threat of moving the White Sox to Seattle can be equally destructive to our larger social identity. Chicagoans knew what happened to New York. Taking the Giants out of New York and the Dodgers out of Brooklyn can be linked with other losses such as the city's financial woes and the shame that New Yorkers suffer under the crumbling image of a once great city—a city that was once the haven for the weary and homeless European and is now the butt of international jokes instead of the locus of personal pride.

A team weaves a history with its city that gives both a personality which cannot be replaced anymore than we can replace an ethnic restaurant with a MacDonald's or a neighborhood bar with a Holiday Inn. When city planners, multi-national corporations and greedy enterpreneurs rev up their bulldozers and swing their wrecking ball in order to pour eight-car-lane slabs of concrete through neighborhoods that give meaning to life and gave us our identity or roots in place and time, a people can be traumatized. A city is interaction: the teams we cheered or wept for; the churches we prayed in; the museums that lifted us from the monotony of life; the public squares and places where people gathered. Somehow they tell us who we are and pull our life together as a people.

Destroy these monuments—our stadiums, our parks, our cathedrals—and you destroy us as a people. The wrecker's ball wipes out the sacred memories of a past that may not have been a succession of "happy" events, but it is ours—more than the clothing we wear. Interstate highways, the Big Mack, and the World's Innkeeper do not evoke the earthy feelings that come from the city streets, the neighborhood hangouts and the sandlot ball parks.

We need to recognize the self-affirming feelings which are evoked by public buildings, the streets, the parks, the schools, the churches, the homes of our neighborhoods and cities before we can understand the sadness or anger that comes upon us when we see the wrecker's crew demolish our sacred citadel of meaningful experiences. It helps us to understand the human response of Jesus as he wept at the thought of the destruction of the city of his love, Jerusalem. Do we grieve over our cities by throwing rocks as people do in South Boston as they feel their Holy City is being destroyed? Can we find more constructive ways to grieve without condoning racism and bigotry? How can we authentically express our compassion?

* * *

I sat next to a middle-aged black woman at the reception in the parish hall after the first mass of a black priest. She knew the young man as a boy in the neighborhood, the church and her kitchen. Her hostility to the church began to trickle out and then flow in a steady stream. She did not go to the first mass or visit the upstairs parish church in ten years. When they started to tamper with the mass, she turned it off. She was a convert, but not baptized into a church that tries to be like a Baptist church. Each of us have heard the Irish, Polish, Italian version of this story. St. Patrick's or St. Rocco's statue was taken out of the sanctuary and put in an out of the way place. No rosary, no benediction, none of the things that made you feel religious are left.

It is easy for a liturgist or gung-ho reformer to put these people down with historical or pastoral arguments to show them how much the new way is better for them. It is more difficult to let them articulate the loss of their childhood or early adult religious rootings. They are saying that the religious forms that held life together are gone. The present symbols do not express for them the reasons for living or the meaning of life. They are in sorrow over the loss of a childhood faith that was mediated by a neighborhood parish church. When Vatican II charted the theology of the Universal Church and began to root out superstition and to search for relevance in a scientific society, the day in and day out life of the ordinary Catholic was cut adrift. Hence the anger of the black woman next to me who is at the same time loving the young man ordained into this "fallen-away-church" as she is spitting out her pain that it no longer cares about her religious experience, so significant at the time of her conversion to Catholicism. We need to understand how the rhythm and forms of a ritual can coincide and support one's own inner rhythms and forms of life. To destroy the one is to destroy the other. This understanding is needed to understand the grief Catholics have experienced since the radical surgery of Vatican II. Grieve she must, but is not a decade long enough? When will she move forward? Who will help her?

* * *

Some of the best times many of us have had has been at weddings. We were choked up as we listened to the couples pledge themselves in sickness and in health till death do them part. The kissing of the bride, the flash bulbs popping, the dinner, the dancing and the noise, escalating in proportion to the traffic at the bar are the precious memories that the couple takes with them into their married life. With an increasingly large number of couples these joyous moments fade and swell into an inferno, a life they can no longer bear. The pain of separating, the agony of being unloved, is then heaped upon their already intense, shared misery. For sincere people, the election to divorce is far from being the "easy way out." The loss of a spouse through divorce is as final and as profound as a loss through death. The despair, the ambivalence, the incredible sorrow are expressed over and over again. Writes Joseph Epstein in *Divorced in America* (Dutton): "A court of divorce. You are standing in a puddle, and there is no solace in having touched bottom. It took you ten years to get there—ten years for the deepest attachment you have known thus far in your life to weaken, then go sour, next turn mean, and now to end in a legal charade.

"The feelings roiling within you are too many and too complicated to be sorted out with any clarity. You want out, and soon—in a matter of minutes, really—you shall have what you want. But you don't feel anything like having arrived at a goal long sought. Instead you feel confused, drained, and somehow, rather cheapened. Even at this moment, going right down to the wire, there are flashes of doubt; these are checked and waved aside. Doubt about this divorce is a luxury whose time has passed. What you want is not so much to be divorced as to have *been* divorced—to have gotten the bloody thing over with."

What does one do with the wedding pictures? It is not different for the priest who leaves the active ministry after a decade or two of relating as a father figure to a flock who depended upon him for their ritual contact with God and people. What does he do with his ordination pictures, his chalice, his symbolic garb that set him aside as a man of the cloth, a public man of God for all people? What feelings emerge when he sits in the pews and listens to boring homilies or witnesses a celebrant who has no celebrative class? In the case of the separated spouse or the priest who has offered his last public Mass, there may indeed be the elation of being freed from a lifestyle but there is a significant loss of an identity that was part of one's self image and history.

For both, their lifestyle was the source of warmth, intimacy, well-being and fulfillment. There is now a significant loss which opens a Pandora's Box of feelings: anger, guilt, anguish, hurt, loneliness, disbelief, loss of status. The hopes and dreams of marital bliss and the messianic hopes of a newly ordained priest may have died a slow death and the loss experienced very gradually, but there is always a terminal date like death itself.

What is Christmas like for the newly divorced? One cannot avoid the jingle-bell music, the crowded stores, the endless number of people who shake hands, nod or smile with an aggressive "Merry Christmas." The recipient may feel like saying "drop dead" or punching the well-wisher in the nose but with masked feelings responds with a smile and "A Merry Christmas to you!" What is it like for the divorced parent on Christmas Eve, alone for the first time without the family, or opening gifts with children who are happily greedy and simultaneously sad, questioning or angry over the absence of a parent? Where do you file the memories of past Christmases, full of gaiety and laughter, warmth and love?

What emotions well up during the lovely Christmas liturgy turned anniversary requiem? What happens to the ritual Christmas dinner when the focus is on an empty chair? How do you deal with in-laws, parents, grandparents—all with advice, blame and poignant reminders of happier days? How do you establish yourself amid the complications of re-marriage. With what do you anchor yourself against the undercurrents in unknown waters? How can you start fresh and anew with stepchildren, alimony, and ingrained customs?

Christmas is the season where losses are most poignantly experienced. Alcoholic excesses and the acting out of hostile feelings as the holiday wears on fills the emergency rooms of our neighborhood hospitals the day after. Families which have experienced recent family losses cannot wait until work and school resume so that the painful feelings can be drugged by the routine or monotony of the daily chores of living. The simple recognition of these feelings as being unrelieved grief is therapeutic. But the recognition itself is a painful effort. It seems somehow easier to deny as camouflage emotional losses rather than look at them squarely. But reality will out and the enemy is better identified than lurking unseen.

* * *

The losses which are most easily identifiable are the physical ones. The Chicago Fire Department employs a therapist as a member of the burn unit to help families deal with the psychic or emotional disturbances to the severely burned victim and the family in which the damaged person lives. Agony haunts many homes. Anguish isolates the sufferer even from those whom he loves and needs. There is the picture of a man whose face is badly scarred, colorated, and puffed up who refuses to leave his home lest he be seen. The newly blinded or those experiencing the gradual loss of sight can be driven into hiding, even locking themselves in the bathroom at the sound of a visitor at the door. In their self-inflicted prison chamber they can pray that the Lord will mercifully deliver them from the pain of living. There is a melancholy litany of the physical and social disabilities which shake people's self-confidence and devastate their self-image that they live lives of desperation or hostility toward the world. Who will mourn with these people? Who will extricate them from the pit of despair they are digging for themselves?

A mother related how she visited faithfully her young son who was institutionalized in the State's most modern facility for which no tax dollar was spared for schooling, testing, and therapy. She was delighted at the humanness and professionalism of the new institution. She visited faithfully during the week and took her son home weekends. The resident children she met were delighted at her many appearances during the week, but they assured her son that she would forget him after awhile and like their parents soon not visit at all. The parents gradually let go of the pain of frequent visits and let the state's professional workers do all the parenting. The loss of the expected normal child and the cost of loving the imperfect child was more than they could handle over the long haul. We said that losses, large and small, were a daily occurrence. As integral components of life, they must be dealt with and they must be seen in context. The opposite of denying one's emotions is not to wallow in them. Rather, the grief process moves a person, rhythmically, through sorrow and into a fuller capacity for joy.

CHAPTER TWO

From Womb to Tomb

Erick H. Erikson, a famous Harvard psychologist, has popularized "the eight stages of man." He has identified and given names and descriptions of what happens to us as we move from childhood, to adolescence, to young adulthood, middle life and old age. As we go from one stage to another there is the pain of leaving the womb, or what was safe but no longer is functional and the anxiety in identifying with a new stage of life which we have yet to experience. Each move to the next stage has its own trauma, as great as our leaving the womb to experience daylight and being cut off from our source of nourishment.

There are marking points in life when each of us is forced to choose a fork in the road. We can no longer pursue the same path in the same way. If we want to have an identity of our own we have to choose a type of work and make decisions that will painfully separate us from the dream of always keeping our options open. We may have to make a choice between the warmth and comfort of a home that provides the security of clean laundry, bed, food, and parents' concern, whose overprotectiveness we resent—or moving away from parents and making it on our own. The playboy or swinger may desire the security of a permanent relationship, but the thought of not being free can immobilize him as he struggles with the choice of depth or breadth.

The agony of moving from one stage to another involves real loss. It means risking the security of the nest for the insecurity of the flight to the unknown. Parents experience the losses of their children from the time a four-year old can say, "I hate you, Mummy." It happens before the child can speak, when the child can feed itself and throws the spoon on the floor in protest. When the child is going through its own form of grief, there may be tantrums and striking out because of the loss of parental help that is being violently rejected. Just because the next step is our own choice it does not mean that we do not try to penalize the people for the losses we suffer. We slay the bearers of bad news; those who provoke us to move from our perch. We want to punish them for our choices that bring us loss.

Parents may get hooked in the beginning, but if they have enough children, enough time, and have dealt well with their own personal losses, they can sit back and watch their children pout. They may volunteer to help them pack and drive them to the bus station when they threaten to leave home because of parental tyranny. Since children mirror adult behavior, reflection on how their children handle loss may be insightful for adults as they come to terms with their own losses.

The mid-life crisis for a man, or male menopause, comes as he gradually slips from the Trying Twenties, to the Hanging-In-There Thirties to the Forlorn Forties. He did not get the promotion he thought the company was grooming him for. He had to go to the police station when he received the call that his daughter was being held for the possession of marijuana. Added to that the plumbing is not functioning after he spent a Saturday working on it. All the while his wife is helping him change his vocabulary from insights she picked up at her women's rap group. The changes in the church may be nothing compared with the implication of changing from chairman to chairperson. Any one of these events can be the shot that is heard around the neighborhood and drive him to the hair stylist, weight-watchers or an ecounter group. Or any combination of which could be a way to prop up his sagging ego.

However, he may choose another route. There is withdrawal to the bottle to be a solitary drinker or to the bar where he finds companionship in his misery or the arms of a more understanding and younger lover. Or it may be a simple coronary thrombosis, the most respectable of all cop-outs. It seems understandable that only a slight proportion of people would be able to identify what is happening to them as the bubble of their dream bursts. Fewer would be able to stay with the pain and ride it out. Easier to choose a target and shoot it out with an external enemy than say: "I must begin to reshape my dream or dream a new dream that fits a man of forty."

One of the weaknesses of the pastoral care departments of our theology schools and hospitals is their inability to see how much of our grief stems from the values of our free enterprise system. While we apply the tourniquet to the limb of the bleeding patient and bind the wound, we must be able to look at the system that causes the patient to bleed. If caring people are not willing to identify the destructive or sinful elements in our society, they become part of the system that bleeds the people we are attempting to heal. This was behind the question put to the saintly Mother Teresa of Calcutta: "What are you doing about the system that perpetuates this poverty?" While we can understand her inability to deal with the question, we as caring people must see our social responsibility to alleviate, not simply the surface pain and grief, but social causes of pain and grief.

In middle life when a man is lying flat on his back with the coronary unit monitoring his heart beat, he can reflect upon the value system that brought him to the hospital in an ambulance. The primary motivation of our capitalist society is profit for the company and the acquisition of material goods for individuals. Competition by definition sets up winners and losers. One loss does not mean a failure any more than a raindrop means a shower, but a school system, an upwardly mobile neighborhood, and a fiercely competitive office, production or sales force can combine to set up a loser or rejection syndrome for the bottom half. This system is built on a class that rules and a class that is ruled. The loser class indulges in cynicism, frustration, apathy or singles out a decade like the sixties to scare hell out of the winner class and then go back to the more comfortable patterns of quiet boredom.

One of the grief producing practices of industry which needs to be looked at is the moving of families around the country like a General Motors Spare Parts Division. With enough pressure from the powers-that-be, and enough ambition to succeed at any cost, the family itself may develop an internalized U-Haul or moving-van syndrome and accept the role of being a company spare part. The U-Haul family never stays long enough to develop lasting relationships. For a long time, the energy required to set up and tear down camp exhausts the family's emotional resources and hides their lack of meaningful pursuits. The result is a litany of losses which, by now, are classic: the high school junior who has her first steady after six different schools and many years of insecurity and rejection; the boy who is doing well in sports or studies and must walk away from his team, his curriculum and start over—again; the wife who must relinquish her status in the community or who never lets herself become involved because of the pain in the last move; the neighborhoods filled with people passing each other like ships in the night, communities of transients—a contradiction in terms!

The Friendly Skies of United becomes the umbilical cord that holds together the extended family. Long distance wires serve as pulsing arteries for clans who cannot even gather at Christmas time if the machinists strike or the checkbook is lean. Jet travel cannot compensate for the day-to-day relations that need the constancy of years to develop into intimate relations that sustain life at the deepest levels. School counselors, attendance officers, clergymen and therapy groups all bear witness to their front-line encounters with the casualties of the campaign. When success and profits are the prize, the path of destruction is wide.

Equally destructive, even devastating, is the loss of a job. A friend called to tell me he lost his job. He had made it financially until the recession came. Like a thief in the night, it took away a high paying, prestigious job from him. On the shady side of middle life, a mortgage commensurate with his job, a notion of his importance, a sizeable family still in school, he was asking himself "Why?" In his brooding moments alone he wanted to know who was to blame for his life which was tumbling down. The target for one's hostility ultimately becomes oneself and one easily slips into depression.

Another dimension of the same problem is the woman who finds her career, her talents and her development all denied or relegated to second-class status due to the upward mobility of her husband's job. With children largely grown up a woman suffers the loss of her very identity when she feels compelled, forced to abandon all in a transfer to yet another city, another promotion for her husband.

What happens to one's self-image as one goes through a long period of self-destructive and self-accusatory idleness? What happens inside to an American male who was brought into the American value system that says that the highest value in life is economic success which provides unlimited education, and care for his children? Calvinistic theology which was appropriated by the family of Catholic immigrants told him that God showed his approval in proportion to his material acquisitions. He had worked hard to get on top. Where is God now? How guilty he must feel for failing his wife, his children, and himself!

Retirement is another source of grief. Why are people who are satisfied with their work, relate well with fellow workers, supervisors and customers, suddenly ostracized because there is an arbitrary retirement age? The desk or work space, the people we have interacted with for thirty years and whom we counted or were counted on by us for humor, cynicism, caring, arguing, or offering a helping hand are gone. The skills that make us who we are, the status that comes simply from age or being "the clown" or wiseman are wiped out by a decree from on high. It all ends on a certain day. The place, job, and people we enjoyed complaining about, our home away from home and relief from family problems have been arbitrarily taken away.

In fantasy the retiree may feel confined to the four walls of a home and to be a twenty-four-hour-a-day partner in a relationship that seemed to work because they were separated for the best part of the day. At the retirement party he/she is given the gold watch treatment. In the "this is your life" program everyone is trying to ease the pain of separation with gifts, humor, kind words; but deep down as the retiree responds with a speech about the long awaited desire to take long vacations, golf, fish, and do all the things one fantasized while working, feels the knot in the stomach from being at the preview of one's own wake. One reads in the paper that the mortality rate is death two years after retirement.

The retiree may feel like a friend of mine, when his family and friends were enjoying a gala party celebrating his sixtieth birthday, who turned to me and in a subdued tone saying, "I don't see anything to celebrate." Obviously his friends were celebrating the beauty of the life they shared with him. To the contrary, the birthday party, at least at this moment, was his way of counting the decade or two that was left, rather than the six that were being celebrated by his friends who reveled in their rich memories of him. There is a real grief that must be acknowledged when a person faces the ending of his life-long work or the significant decreasing of his mathematical life-expectancy. Glitter and gaiety are shallow substitutes for the concern and recognition necessary when one passes into another stage of life.

The "stages of man" or marking points in life need to be seen in their cultural setting. In our American youth culture the loss of youth is a horrendous issue from the appearance of the first gray hair to the feeling of loss of vitality. It can prompt all kinds of disruptive behavior including suicide. Our TV and newspaper ads tell us that to be young is to be beautiful. When have you last seen a book cover at the air terminal newsrack with an elderly person seated in a rocking chair with a glow of well-being? Old age does not stimulate our fantasy life enough to sell products. America tells us we should feel sorry for ourselves as we age.

While not being used to sell wares may be one of the blessings of old age, it is indeed one of the traps we set for every American who still believes him or herself to be young, but particularly women who have made a career of being chic. How is a woman going to view herself as she loses her cosmetic beauty, when her wrinkles cannot be ironed out and her gray hair can only be turned to blue? How does our society prepare women for the real truth about what Revlon, the Avon Lady and Helena Ruben-stein can do for them? The truth may be revealed in the midst of fun and games with friends, a look in the mirror in the morning when many other parts of our life are not functioning well, or the innocent remark of a child. In the Christian tradition the revelation of the truth about life has never been confined to the Bible. What do we do with these discoveries?

The tragic treatment of our aged is reflected in the frequent news reporting of the latest nursing home scandal.

The Boston Globe, December 29, 1975, carried a first page feature article: "Relatives Rob Elderly in Rest Homes."

A relative will show a check to the patient and say, 'This is for you Auntie. It's a government check . . . Just

41

sign it on the back.' She'll sign the check, thanking him for bringing it. He'll say, 'Here's $5 for you, dear . . . I'll take care of you because I love you.' And he'll leave with the $25, not to return for a month. . . .

Relatives who abscond with such funds acquire the money because their victims are either too mentally incompetent to perceive they are being denied their money, or too insecure to complain.

Sixty-three percent of the nursing home patients in New England are on Medicaid that gives them this $25 monthly. Here is the final indignity that old folks must suffer, not at the hands of an impersonal government, a nursing-home-for-profit, but the benign and not-so benign neglect of one's own family. The nursing home is the American symbol for what happens when the American dream of eternal youth is punctured. It stands as a national monument in a nation-wide cemetery to the ruthlessness of an economic and social system that grinds people on the downward slope of life in a process not unlike an electric disposal unit—only a little less antiseptic than Orwell's 1984.

Unlike the X-rays which show us our terminal cancer or the televised electrocardiac waves we can watch from our bedside, we can easily deny old age. New clothes, new cosmetics, new lifestyles are only the superficial ways in which we deny the aging process at work in us. Probably the barometer of our comfortableness with the aging going on in our-selves is our comfortableness with aging people. Does their age, their feebleness, their withdrawal from our own interests create anxiety in us which keeps them hiding in their closet lest they meet with our feelings of avoidance of them. We treat the aged as people with a communicable disease rather than as people who can mirror the process that brings *us* to the wheel chair and being spoon fed after a stroke, like a baby. No one is saying unequivocally that old age is beautiful, but there are enough exceptions to know that it can be a period of completion or fulfill-ment for people who have the courage to recognize their loss of life day-by-day.

It seems easier to deal with sudden blindness, loss of hearing, or serious illness which is identifiable by medics or can be researched in medical libraries than the aging process. Other than the retirement from work or the breaking up of one's household because of the inability to do the minimum chores of an efficiency apartment there are few clear markers in the aging process which are stop lights that say: "You are living an illusion. You must look at the daily losses in your life which, though imperceptible now, are going to demand their toll not simply in physical impairment of faculties but on your self-image. The rest of the world is looking at you as aged. How do you look at yourself in your declining years? Are you becoming spiritually, physically, richer or poorer? Are you becoming more joyful or more bitter? Look beneath the wrinkles under your eyes and examine the state of your soul?

The crochetiness and anger of elderly people results from people who in midlife, did not come to terms with what is happening to their outlook on life. It is due to a narrowness of vision which hampers their perception of the Spirit moving creatively, broadly, through the world. A Spirit who inspires new generations to plant and harvest, new ideas and dreams to hatch. In the absence of omens warning of biological malfunctioning, the aging man or woman can somehow evade the stark reality of being finite, limited. The bitterness and cynicism of the aged may well be related to physical impairment of the nervous system, but it should not be a shield for those on the ski slope denying old age as they slide into the valley of darkness.

It is in the valley of darkness that we meet death. Do we see death as a friend or foe? Is it the grim reaper or the angel of deliverance? In the Victorian era death was something people could talk about while sex was a taboo. In our time sex became table talk and death an obscenity. Dr. Elizabeth Kubler-Ross has helped us to talk about death as we do the equally elemental reality of birth. One evening on TV, I saw a family experience a beautiful death of an old friend at a New Year's party and a news documentary of a popular course taught at a college where students simulated their own death and burial, including lying in a coffin. The course was designed to provide vicarious experiences of death so that students might become aware of the shortness of life and thus define their own in terms of death.

Americans are still light years away from accepting death and wearing it like an old shoe as do our European ancestors. As a hospital chaplain I entered a room in which two patients were laughing as they were regaling themselves in conversation, which they quickly shared with me. The Lithuanian-born occupant of the room was a terminal cancer patient. She and her patient-visitor were talking about what kind of a second wife her husband should choose after her death. Her preference was a woman who would come with him once a month to put a flower on her grave. She went on to tell joyously about the good times she had as a child on Sundays when the family would picnic at the family cemetery. She saw death as a friend and which also opened up new possibilities for the husband she dearly loved. Since we Americans have not been brought up in Eastern European cemeteries or enjoyed the conviviality of Irish wakes which makes death a staple of life like bread and tea, students are taking weird courses to discover death as they would flying saucers.

Death is the only loss from which nothing can be salvaged. Divorce is like death but in many ways potentially more painful because the tender and painful moments of the past can be awakened at the sight of the former spouse whom one sees when he or she exchange greetings at the time of the visitation of the children. However, death has a distinctive quality of utter finality. Unlike the professional skier who has lost the use of limbs but has the possibility of building a new world of meaning, when there is the official medical pronouncement of death, there is a finality like nothing else. Death is the most irreparable of losses.

Death is more easily seen as a friend than a foe when it has been anticipated by a *full* life. When the patient has suffered a long, incurable illness it is seen as a merciful deliverance, the answer to prayers. The Quinlan case has forced the American people to see that length of days through machine-induced life may not be a truly human response to the gift of life. Rather it becomes a denial of God's promise of a new and better life. The case put the Catholic tradition on the limitations of science in the face of genuine human and religious values on trial before the American people. Is death to be treated as an evil? Is the preservation of biological life to be maintained at all cost as the highest value in life?

There are two sets of losses which need to be

distinguished: the loss of one's own life, and the deaths of significant people in our own life. Obviously they are related. If we are comfortable with the thought of our own dying, we can more easily accept the deaths of those we love.

The two most potentially significant losses that a human suffers are the deaths of the two parental figures in one's life. If the parent dies before the offspring has had the time or opportunity to separate him or herself emotionally and physically from one's family or origin, then the loss can be a complete shattering of one's world and take years to repair. The opposite may be true when the parent is aged and the offspring are middle-aged.

The minister can never be sure how the bereaved will relate to the death of their "loved" one as he or she enters the funeral parlor. I was about to offer my sympathies to a woman in middle life who was burying a mother who had lived vigorously until close to death in her eighties. The daughter caught the somber, professional look of sadness of my face and with a smile that lighted up her whole face told me that this was not an occasion for the expression of sympathy because this was the celebration of the beautiful life of her mother. She caught me in my act of professional mourning, so we laughed. The loss through death of her mother was an event she had been experiencing day-by-day during the decade the mother had given up her apartment to move into the home of her daughter. In the jargon of pastoral psychology this is called anticipatory grief. The grieving is long finished before the event that actualizes the loss takes place.

Death, obviously, is inevitable. The emotionally healthy person will be better equipped to cope with death, her own or another's, simply because she has not denied its reality. And it is this same reality which we face when we grapple with the endless smaller losses of daily life. This grappling, this struggle into maturity, is the frontier where we discover new dimensions of our beliefs. It is the climb by which we gain perspective. Death is more than an end. It is also a passage and a beginning. When we are finished mourning, it *is* appropriate to celebrate!

CHAPTER THREE

The Grief Process

The name that is associated internationally with the popularization of the grief process is Dr. Elizabeth Kubler-Ross. She is a Swiss-born psychiatrist who examines not simply the symptoms of the dying patient but the feelings of these people as they walk through the valley of darkness. She has been able to describe for the helping professions, through her countless lectures and her book *On Death and Dying*, the stages through which a person passes as one comes to terms with one's own death. This writer attended the weekly interviews of dying patients which she conducted with the assistance of the chaplain's staff of the University of Chicago Hospitals in 1969-70 (of which I was a member).

Grief is a catch-all word for the feelings and altered behavior that one experiences from a significant loss. It describes the state one enters from a loss that somehow touches upon one's self-image, personhood, or social and family systems. Grief is a prism through which one's life is filtered until the loss has been integrated into a new life pattern.

The grief process is the movement through which one lives as one experiences the loss day by day. Hopefully it is a healing process as one goes through this psychic movement from one state of being to another. It must be emphasized that grief is not pathological but a healthy response to the ebb and flow of life. What Kubler-Ross and others are saying is that we now have much data from case histories that helps us to identify the feelings and psychic behavior as one moves through grief from the moment it comes to awareness until it finds resolution.

Grief-work or the management of grief is a term for the facilitation of the process. It emphasizes the discipline, art, or professional stance the helping professions are taking toward grief in our times. As we shall see, particularly with acute grief, the helping people need more skills than simply physical presence and pious words. Grief-work is a task that can require a large commitment of time and well-honed psychological insights and ministry skills. This work goes on before the person comes to the final healing stages where it may be seen as the loving hand of God. When grief-workers become irritated at the easy "God loves you" approach of the all-things-to-all minister, it is not because of the minister's piety but because of his naivete in not realizing that with a serious loss the grief-worker needs to do more than give a person a pious pat. Helping people work through their acute grief is indeed an art.

Bereavement is often viewed narrowly as the state of the person after the death of a person who is loved, highly prized or held very dear. When we see a boy or girl suffering from acne after their steady has deserted them or a young adult has a puffy face and is red in the eyes from nights of crying over the breaking of an engagement, we do not refer to them as bereaved, but the sorrow is physically visible. Physically and emotionally they are all in real pain.

The classic research on grief, however, has not been done with the wide variety of losses or little deaths we have described in Chapter One and Two but has been done by studying the effects of death on the bereaved in the traditional sense of the word. But these studies are still basic to an understanding of the psycho-dynamics of every form of sorrow, whether it be personal, social or familial.

Psychologists have zeroed in on one of these losses, namely the loss of life of a very significant figure in our life. In 1942, a team of Harvard psychiatrists under Dr. Erich Lindemann interviewed 101 patients who had suffered the loss of a relative under a number of circumstances including the Coconut Grove fire in Boston. These scientists carefully studied the results and from it came an article in the *American Journal of Psychiatry* entitled "The Symptomatology and Management of Acute Grief." This is a landmark study that has added, "grief-work," "the grief process" and the "management of grief" to our medical, psychological and pastoral jargon. I live in a community of ministry students where we say jocosely to anyone at the table who looks depressed, "what are you 'into grief' about?" The new terminology is simply a sophisticated way of talking about "living with sorrow." Enabling people to move out of their grief is a labor of love that is measured in hours, days, weeks, months, and years. Somehow our Puritan ethic insists that it be labeled work rather than love.

If we look at some of the findings of Lindemann we will recognize the spectrum of grief symptoms, diffused and less intense, in all of the losses people suffer. The cause of the grief is not the main indicator. Rather, the degree of grief suffered is a measure of the degree of re-integration necessary in the personality. The minister or helper must be sensitive to the pain of adjustment in each concrete situation. The pain can be very real even if it appears unjustified by circumstance.

Some of the somatic symptoms of acute grief are: "sensations of somatic distress occurring in waves lasting from twenty minutes to an hour at a time, a feeling of tightness in the throat, choking with shortness of breath, need for sighing, an empty feeling in the abdomen, lack of muscular power, and an intense subjective distress described as tension or mental pain."

This discomfort can be precipitated by visits, by mentioning the deceased and by receiving sympathy. There is a tendency to avoid the syndrome at any cost—to refuse visits lest they should precipitate the reaction, and to keep deliberately from all thoughts and references to the deceased. Some can feel that they are going insane. For example, the young navy pilot who lost a close friend with whom he continued to eat and talk over his problems. Even six months after the death he would not admit that his friend was no longer with him.

"One of the big obstacles to this work," writes Lindemann, "seems to be the fact that many patients try to avoid both the intense distress connected with the grief experience and the necessary expression of emotion. The male victims bereaved by the Coconut Grove fire appeared in the early psychiatric interviews to be in a state of tension, with tightened facial musculature, unable to relax for fear they might 'break down.' They required considerable persuasion to yield to the grief process which would enable them to accept the discomfort of bereavement . . . they became willing to accept the grief process and to embark on a program of dealing in memory with the deceased person. As soon as this change was accomplished there seemed to be a rapid relief of tension, and the subsequent interviews were rather animated conversations in which the deceased was idolized and in which misgivings about the future adjustment were worked through."

Not all psychosomatic illnesses with which doctors are confronted deal with bereavement from the death of a loved one. Many are from very ordinary losses such as the separation from one's family. At the local University Hospital there is a somatic illness humorously called the Windemere syndrome. It is named for the Hotel at which many of these patients reside. The typical patient is an elderly matron who lives with other elderly matrons at the Windemere, the lobby of which is lined every afternoon with well-dressed dowagers sitting by themselves quietly or talking in pairs.

These are women who have raised families which have in turn migrated to the suburbs to raise families of their own. Their married children form a rim of thirty miles around the hotel. In these suburban communities they are the backbone of the Citizens for Better Living, the PTA's, the Chambers of Commerce, United Fund Drive, Catholic Charities committees and the local committee for Bonds for Israel.

When mother goes to see her doctor she complains about two things which are the doctor's quick way of identifying the Windemere syndrome. She intertwines a description of where the pain is and how much it hurts with chatter about the traffic nowadays on those expressways and how no one can travel them anymore. The doctor proceeds with the physical and finds nothing wrong, so on the second visit he suggests that she might go to the hospital for a thorough check-up. The woman is quite eager and then there is more talk about traffic on the expressways.

When she is tucked away in the hospital bed, traffic really picks up. A four alarm call goes to every suburb in which there is an uncle, aunt, brother, sister, but especially where there is a son or daughter and grandchildren. There is an upswing in the sale and delivery of get-well cards, business picks up with the local florist. The whole family is rallying to a crisis built on the guilt they feel for neglecting mother.

All the meetings they had on the calendar must be cancelled until they get the final word on mother's tests. The quality of suburban education and the funding for local projects will take a nose dive in this period, but what are they compared with feelings about mother.

The Windemere syndrome tests at the hospital always prove inconclusive. The doctor never says that mother is not dying but that the tests don't show anything that would justify her staying in the hospital any longer. This is a relief to the family. They vow that they will never leave mother alone again after all the heart rending descriptions of life in the Windemere that she was able to fill them in on during their visits. They vow they will visit her at the Windemere frequently. They will send in grandchildren to stay with her overnight on occasion. They will put aside their feelings on finding her a nuisance to have around and bring her back and forth for visits more frequently. Everyone seems happy and the pains are gone. The whole episode was well worth the price. The family is re-united. Mother is still the umbilical cord that unites the clan.

But tensions at home do build up and the expressways seem to get clogged with traffic, the trip again becomes long and tedious, the telephone calls become less frequent through the year, grandchildren come but they are not so eager and the visits are briefer and less frequent.

Finally the traffic to the Windemere is slowed to a virtual halt and mother is having pains again. She goes to the same doctor two or three years later talking about pains and traffic and he plays the script the way it is written. Mother sends out the guilt messages and a delinquent family comes in penitent fashion to a mother who has made them feel rotten.

The Windemere syndrome is simply mother's brand of unresolved grief over the loss of affection and attention she had enjoyed while in the mainstream of the family. It may seem quite minor, but for her it is painfully real. Only the outsider perceives the comic relief it offers from the intensely tragic. In a more artificial situation, the postponed or unresolved grief or a sudden, fatal loss can wreak tremendous havoc. The delay of the grief reaction results in bizarre morbid effects and even death itself to the one who cannot grieve.

"The delayed reactions," according to Lindemann, "may occur after an interval which was not marked by any abnormal behavior or distress, but in which there developed an *alteration* in the party's conduct, perhaps not conspicuous or serious enough to lead him to a psychiatrist . . . the manifestations may be classified as follows: (1) *overactivity without a sense of loss* rather with a sense of activities being of an expansive and adventurous nature and bearing semblance to the activities formerly carried out by the deceased . . . (2) *the acquisition of symptoms belonging to the last illness of the deceased.* This type of patient is seen in medical clinics and the ailment is often labeled hypochondriasis or hysteria. . . . There is another type of disorder no doubt presenting (3) a recognized medical disease, namely, a group of psychosomatic conditions, predominately ulcerative colitis rheumatoid arthritis, and asthma. Extensive studies in ulcerative colitis have produced evidence that 33 out of 41 patients with ulcerative colitis developed their disease in close relationship to the loss of an important person. Indeed, it was this observation that first gave the impetus for present detailed study of grief. . . .

"At the level of social adjustment there often occurs a conspicuous (4) alteration in relationship to friends and relatives. The patient feels irritable, does not want to be bothered, avoids former social activities, and is afraid he might antagonize his friends by his lack of interest and his critical attitudes. . . .

"While overflowing hostility appears to be spread out over all relationships, it may also occur as (5) *furious hostility against specific persons*. . . . (6) Many bereaved persons struggle with much effort against these feelings of hostility, which to them seem absurd, representing a vicious change in their characters that must be hidden as much as possible. Some patients succeed in hiding their hostility but become wooden and formal, with affectivity and conduct *resembling schizophrenic symptoms*. . . . (7) Closely related to this is a lasting loss of patterns of social interaction.

"The patient cannot initiate any activity, is full of eagerness to be active, is restless and cannot sleep, but through the day he will not start any activity unless primed by somebody else." Such patients may be active but are detrimental to their own social and economic existence by plunging into foolish economic schemes or "stupid acts" that alienate their friends. It is self-punitive behavior without any awareness of excessive feelings of guilt.

The most disasterous symptom is *"agitated depression* with tension, agitation, insomnia, feelings of worthlessness, bitter self-accusation and obvious need for punishment. Such patients may be dangerously suicidal."

While the intensity of interaction with the deceased before his death seems to be significant, the interaction does not have to be of the affectional type. It may be the death of a person who invited much hostility that could not well be expressed because his status or claim to family loyalty. Thus two middle-aged men were overheard in a hospital corridor discussing the rapidly approaching hour of death of their elderly father, a person they experienced as a wealthy, self-centered hateful old tyrant. They had instructed the medical staff to spare no pains or cost in prolonging their father's life—a procedure carried out with the usual oxygen masks, blood transfusions, drugs, intravenous feedings, and succession of operations. As death drew near, one said to the other: "They really gave it to the old blank, blank, blank, didn't they." They did not love their father, but hated him and used the useless hospital procedures to spit out their poison. The loss of their father was significant and the occasion for acting out their grief in this cruel way. The loss of an object of hate can leave a vacuum in one's life network.

Acting out one's hate is not an appropriate way to resolve grief. Hate produces guilt which calls for forgiveness and reconciliation. These men have the choice of projecting their hate for their father on others or changing, with God's help, their relationship with their deceased parent.

We say we grieve over the loss of another, but we really mean that we grieve for ourselves. As we move from childhood on we become a part of our surroundings as we form a network of relationships. This whole context of life becomes ourself, who each of us is. When we lose a part of the physical environment, a close relationship, or a part of our body, then our sense of identity has been damaged. Our self image has been fractured. The whole system needs time to pull itself together. We begin the inner process of evolving into another self. As we move through this evolution the lost friend or home or function is shifted from a position of vital importance and new strengths and energies are able to emerge. It helps to see life as the flow of the river which is always moving, never the same. Life is a process in which death and rebirth are natural and normal. The pain of loss does not make the process less human. Pain and joy, the joy, for instance, of a new relationship being born or an old one being revived, are two sides of the same coin. Good grief is good health, or more simply, being human.

CHAPTER FOUR
Feelings Facilitate

Sorrow is a human response to pain. One who does not grieve lives a less than fully human life. To become human we let it all hang out. We can avoid this pain of grieving by setting our expectations and involvement in life so low that we function as robots rather than persons. The price of avoiding sorrow is to harden one's hearts by withdrawal from relationships, to build a protective shield around us. This is what we are inclined to do when we become overwhelmed with grief. Grief is simply one of the juices of life, without which life is not human. In this chapter we are trying to point up the constructive use of feelings in the grief process.

John Jones is a twenty-six-year-old preparing for ordination to the priesthood. A classmate left his religious community: "How do you feel about it, John?"

"It does not bother me. I have been through this so often that I decided that I would not let it bother me again. One year, ten left, the next year another ten and by two years ago we were down to five from the original thirty."

I invited him to share his feelings. He chose not to. I understood. It would be too painful. For whatever reason this was not the time and place. I felt sad that once again he could not ventilate the feelings that obviously are packed inside and become like a mass of concrete in one's intestines. He felt he had to forego again expressing the feelings of loss and the sharing of destiny he had with his classmates. It did not mean that he had an intimate relationship with a significant number who left, but each was part of the structure of community life, even the ones whom he may have despised. He could not even express his relief at the departures of those he felt were a burden to him.

A little of him died each time a community member left and since as a human being there was grieving going on inside him which he chose not to externalize, it had to be internalized. It could only block other human feelings and stifle his humanity which is the chief tool of the priest or minister. His choice now was to go about with a depressive, hang-dog, "poor me" look of false humility asking people to walk over him or become a silent, aggressive, angry man who pops off at the least provocation. The picture, however, is not totally bleak. The healing Spirit works at his own pace and John may ultimately become the best developed and empathic minister.

It will be after he has "hit bottom" like an alcoholic and then starts and stays with the long process of dealing with his self inflicted emotional scars. He can become the "wounded healer," one emotional cripple ministering to another.

Grief is a visceral affair. We experience it in the gut where we feel a tightness that may be a rage we are trying to hold back, or under the armpits or in palms made sweaty from anxiety that has been repressed for decades, or in the tear ducts that must be drained before life can flow with some serenity. Healthy grief is expressed in feelings. If the feings are genuine, appropriate and congruent, they are expressed in the context of the loss itself, not by biting the head off a store clerk who makes a simple error or going into a tirade over someone who is late for dinner. If the loss is denied on the surface level, it will work its way through subterranean passages. It may become lodged in the viscera and remain there as poison and express itself in a depressive face or by popping out in embarrassing and destructive ways.

One thing we can be sure about is that we do have feelings about significant losses whether we admit it or not. We can go around denying that we are affected with pious phrases about God's will or goodness or toss it off like a gambler with "you win one and you lose one." To deny feelings for a long period is to become a stoic like the Sheriff in *Gunsmoke* who could walk over his dead mother without a tear as he goes out to meet the robbers at the pass, or be a

Nervous Nellie with neurotic and hypochondriac symptoms.

We must ask ourselves if we regard feelings as friends or foes. Southern Europeans tend to regard feelings as friends while Northern Europeans see them as foes, thus our ethnic origins might give us some clues. The teaching of John Calvin has had its influence on the American businessman, Protestant and Catholic. He is taught to play it cool, not get involved in feelings, lest it interfere with his making it rich which is a sign of God's approval.

What we are addressing ourselves to in this chapter is the constructive use of the feelings we experience as we work our way through grief. It means that we must have a conviction that feelings are resources we can draw upon in time of stress rather than enemies that embarrass us and do us in. They are simply nature's tools for bringing us through periods of stress and strain.

The obvious way of relieving our feelings of loss is through tears—simply let the hurt drain off and in the process purge and purify all the blocked passages. Tears may come when denial is broken through or the event has taken place. The deed is done. The divorce decree is finalized. We have moved out of our apartment and into the nursing home. The casket is closed. The Dear John letter is read. But tears don't always come that easily. Our culture and our family patterns have a lot to say about who cries and on what occasions. Men are not allowed to weep in public. In 1972, Senator Muskie ruined his chances to be Presidential nominee when he wept after hearing his wife publicly denounced.

Women are permitted to cry, but not always as is illustrated in this case: Mary who had lost her husband a few years previous goes to her doctor with a long list of physical symptoms. Tests proved negative, but as her story unfolded she told how she had been happily married for forty years. The extremely happy marriage was ended by the sudden death of her husband. She related how she never cried once. Her children reinforced this behavior by telling her how brave and noble she was.

She did not like to talk about her husband. The doctor asked why she did not talk about him if it was such a wonderful marriage. "It was too unpleasant." "Why," he asked, "should it be unpleasant? You said you had forty years of happy marriage, that you were very much in love with your husband, that it was a wonderful relationship? Why do you have to crowd them out of the focus of your attention." She replied, "I'm afraid I might cry." The price for holding back her tears and pleasing her family was three years of physical distress. She finally got her doctor to admit her to the hospital where she cried for three days straight. "I would be lying in bed, thinking about the past and weeping, and the nurse would come in and say, 'Don't be upset honey. Don't cry.' She replied, 'I told her I'm paying for this. I'm going to cry if I want to.' "

Another device to stop people from crying is to hug and hold them when they start. This is done in the name of empathy, but often the comforter is uncomfortable with a person sobbing by themselves. The helping person can hinder nature's healing by not respecting the inner process that has its own timing and rhythm and requires that the comforter allow inner space for the mourner to grieve.

Tears are a release and a relief when they begin to flow and we may feel that the mourning period is over. We would like to computerize the grief process and put our feelings on a production schedule but they are unpredictable. After the catharsis of tears we may be in a rage over the loss, or the rage may anticipate the tears, but as surely as night follows day, anger or rage is going to surface like a hydra-headed monster and act out its feelings before we will find an inner peace. The degree of anger or rage will depend upon a number of variables: the significance of the loss, the need it filled in our security system, the suddenness of the loss, the delay in its recognition, one's family and culture systems or history.

Somewhere between the times of Jesus and present day Catholicism, anger as a positive force in the spiritual life has been lost. Religion teachers taught us that Jesus was meek and mild, a modern, bland Mr. Milquetoast, a proverbial doormat. Anger was something for the confessional like disobedience, impure thoughts, and murder. This perversion of the humanity of Jesus may have come from teachers and parents who like antiseptic classrooms and homes where only smiles or SMILE buttons can be worn on the face or the coat lapel.

Anger is an emotion that may be embarrassing and which we wish would go away. We easily attach guilt to it and place a negative value on it, that is, something bad. A toothache, on the contrary, is something to be rid of, but we do not attach guilt to the pain as we do with anger. Anger, unlike the toothache, may be therapeutic, an agent that facilitates the mourning as we move toward normalcy and to a deeper level of humanity. In anger we say, "I have lost a part of myself. I am shaken, incomplete, insecure, upset." Then we search for a target, any target. It may be the bearer of the bad news, as when Saul killed the messenger who told him his son was killed.

The prime target of displaced anger is our family, the people closest to us, those we feel understand us and somehow will not turn us off completely because we cannot cope. It is a heavy presumption and many of us have experiences of risking an explosion and dumping feelings that belong somewhere else on a friend and having the relation severed for life. This is the risk on both sides. When there is no one we can trust with our anger, then the feeling may not be released and be converted into neurotic or physical symptoms.

Professional people can also be immediate targets. The doctor who made a decision to operate or not to operate can be blamed for the death of a loved one. In fantasy he becomes the killer. The nurse may be held responsible, indeed anyone, for not doing or doing something, the opposite of which would have prevented the tragedy. The best advice to people who are being attacked by the bereaved or the person under seige is to understand the attack as simply frustration, discomfort, or hurt. It is simply the draining of a clogged up system that cannot absorb the waste in the normal way and is backing up and spewing the muck in every direction. So we keep our composure, let the person ventilate until somehow the pressure is off the system and these hostile feelings are drained through work, play, and other ordinary channels of emotional release.

God is a natural dumping ground for hostile feelings and someone whom we can punish for our loss. If he holds the whole wide world in his hands and orders the events of life, then why does he do this to me? What did I do wrong? Why not pick on someone who lives a dissolute life? We can get our heavy artillery out and let God have it. We can stop praying, give up the practice of Sunday Mass, be demanding of others to practice their religion legalistically as a form of punishment as we see ourselves punished. The mind and emotions can be very creative in designing ways of getting even with God.

We need not mind how much people take out their feelings on God because he can take it. No one can hurt God. It is when I am attacked as his surrogate, a man of the cloth, that I scream, holler or go to my therapist or doctor for a remedy. Under attack I am not always inclined to be an authority on the grief process but rather a hurting human being who takes personally what is meant for God or simply the person crying out in pain saying, "Does anyone care about me in my misery?" As a parish priest "I took it for God" when people felt their neighborhood would change from white to black and they would lose their financial, emotional, spiritual and familial security. I was attacked because I identified with the proposition of God, country and church that all men are equal. Everyone believes this proposition until their personal security is endangered. At that time God's visible representative in the community must absorb their anger until they have entered and lived through the grieving or mourning process.

Parents know what it is to stand in for God and take the beating their adolescents intend for God. Who gets the blame for rejection on a date, low grades in school, a reprimand by the basketball coach, for being too short or too tall or too fat or too skinny or having acne? It is the ones who choose to bring this child in the world. This would never have happened if this man and woman did not choose to be parents and bring any of these woes to a high school sophomore. Parents learn to relax and not internalize the blame that goes with the anger and call it the crisis of identity or simply the pains of growing up.

Teachers and other authority figures know that every outburst of anger or act of sullen silence or passive aggression is not personal but is related to some loss in the person's life that he or she is unaware of and has not come to terms with. The authority figure need not play the role of therapist or even comforter or healer but simply not over-react as though the anger was personal rather than someone acting out their grief. They focus on this person because they are not ready to enter the place of pain within themselves and stay with it until it is dissipated.

Anger that is a part of sorrow can be used constructively. It can generate an energy that can redress grievances in society, raise consciousness, and give one the drive to sustain the thrust to achieve these goals for society so that others may not suffer similar losses or ease their pain in the aftermath. "Anger," writes Mel Krantzler in Creative Divorce (Evans), "the fuel required for pulling apart from our past marriages, can continue to alert us to obstacles blocking our growth as independent people. Anger unrecognized takes many forms—sarcasm, apathy, depression, bitterness, hostility. In a creative divorce anger is accepted for what it is and becomes translated into *appropriate action.*"

Blacks, browns, and women who have not been accepted because of race or sex must live with the sorrow of not being recognized as full persons. They can live lives of frustration; hate whitey, gringoes or males or they can put their anger to use in black power, brown power or the women's movements. All social progress or consciousness raising comes from people who have felt the sting of injustice and align themselves with those similarly oppressed to the point of rage or anger and thus do not waste their sorrow. The alcoholic or drug addict who is angry about his past can turn his anger into voluntary service of those who are struggling to overcome their addiction.

Guilt is a feeling that accompanies loss and anger. There is an innate question we ask ourselves after the shock of acknowledgment of the loss. What did I do wrong that I deserve this fate? So we rummage through our guilt bag and try to piece together a case against ourselves that proves us guilty beyond a reasonable doubt. The woman who was sharp with her husband when he left for work on the day he gets killed on the way home "knows" that she is guilty. If it is not that obvious, then we go slowly over the events of our marriage to find the things we did wrong that led to this divorce. It may be the way we dealt with a child who is in trouble with the police, proving that our child training was too strict or too permissive or that if I hadn't blown up at my boss I would never have been fired. I have a need to be the culprit and demand a punishment that no judge would dare inflict on me.

We have been describing neurotic guilt as contrasted with real guilt, which results from the conscious destructive things we do to one another. We cannot easily separate one from the other. At this point, however, we are simply trying to identify guilt as an element in the grief process. Guilt unrecognized or unreconciled for a long period can lead to the somatic and psychic illnesses described in an earlier chapter.

A young man in his early twenties while away at college receives news that his father died suddenly. He came home for the funeral and returned to college without the shedding of a single tear or any show of concern, in spite of the reality that he spent his whole life in a very close affectional and work relationship with his father until a few months before he left home.

A few months after the funeral the young man's life exhibited a drastic change. From an outgoing, joyous person, he became depressed, a loner, lost weight, and preferred study to developing intimate relationships. He rapidly lost weight from not eating and began a long history of somatic illnesses. He blamed himself for his father's death. He interpreted his leaving home as the cause of his father's feelings of rejection by his son which deprived the father of his reason for living. He took upon himself the sin of patricide and choose a life of self-inflicted punishment in the form of prayer, fasting and ill health. He was fortunate to have found in later life a therapist who was able to help him surface feelings about his father. He felt the intervention of the therapist arrested his own early death. The direction of his life was reversed but recovery was slow. There was the deeply rooted low self-esteem and inability to make claims for himself as someone with self-worth. However, with a little help from his friends over the next decade he had come to discover that he had punished himself enough for his foul deed and could enjoy life again as he did as a young man. Without a strong identification with his religious tradition which glorified suffering with the symbol of the cross or Christ crucified plus a strong vocation identity, he may easily have chosen the ultimate or "perfect" form of self-punishment: suicide.

Guilt leads to loneliness, a form of self-exile. Loneliness is a feeling that follows a significant loss. If the person, the relationship, the job, the sport that gave us pleasure was the linchpin of our social system, the key that gave meaning to all other parts of life and kept them in proper relationship to each other, is forever gone or ended, then there is a vacuum in our life—a hole that looks like an abyss. The joy of life which one experiences when everything comes together in some experience is now gone. The food seems to lose its flavor. The television entertainers cease to be funny. The spice of life is gone. The juices are not flowing We take a dim view of life. We are depressed. Even the anticipation of a loss can bring this feeling of loneliness. A friend contemplating divorce was confronted with the thought of having Christmas dinner alone in a hotel dining room. It was presented as a modern version of hell, the symbol of irreparable separation, the epitome of loneliness.

With a death or a divorce the loss or loneliness is often symbolized by a chair in a corner of a room, a trinket here or there that reminds the bereaved of sacred moments of togetherness. These symbols are two-edged swords. They remind us of beautiful moments in the past that can give us courage and stability and they are fetishes that can bind us to the past so tightly that we cannot move on and live in the present. We can sell the house and rid ourselves of the reminders of the dead past or we can live in it as a mausoleum preserving everything intact as though we were waiting for the Second Coming when the deceased or the divorced spouse would walk in the door and life would pick up where it was in the halcyon days. We can find ourselves trapped between holding on to the past or denying the past. Somehow we must find a middle course of accepting our history without its ruling our lives. This is equally true about political life. In Northern Ireland the entire population are still reacting to the Battle of the Boyne as though it were yesterday and pledging undying loyalty to the ghosts of the past. They are victims of their history.

The loneliness of the aged may result in part from too many losses. Their friends have died. There is no one left to share their memories. New people enter their lives but there may not be a willingness on either side to enter relationships at a deep level. Older people can be treated patronizingly. They are invited to all the family gatherings but are not privy any longer to family secrets. It is done in the name of not burdening them with our worries. The result of not permitting them to become involved in family affairs is a form of imprisonment, a sentence to further loneliness.

CHAPTER FIVE

Out of the Confusion Syndrome

When one is in grief, there are feelings of confusion, withdrawal, bursts of anger, low energy, and psychosomatic symptoms described in Chapter Two. If one uses a medical model to describe life, one might describe grief symptoms as illness. However, if one takes a more holistic view of life and sees life as seasons of the year, winters and springs, highs and lows, death and rebirth, then grieving is natural and a part of life as are chilling winds of winter and the hard earth waiting for the Spring thaw and gentle breezes. The joys of life that come with the robins and the flowers in bloom will yield again to the falling leaves and the barren earth as new losses enter our life which will wait again for another spring. The grief is not a sickness to be cured but a natural death to a part of us that we must shed and transcend so that the new life that is under the surface may blossom in ways that have not been developed in our personhood. The model is not sickness and health but death to old styles and birth to a new part of us, simply a way of describing the life process.

The pain, the confusion, the withdrawal, the

anger must be channeled in such a way that we can look at it. While this is normally done by talking or writing about it, it is also done by hitting a pillow until the feathers are all over the room, crying and sighing, or long periods of prayerful reflection.

We need some structure to the process of pulling it together so that our minds and hearts become one, our reason and our emotions are in tune with each other. We offer three structures: our story, a friend, the community. Hopefully all of them available and used at the same time. Ultimately we have to pull it all together in a story. A wise person writes: "All sorrows can be borne if you put them into a story or tell a story about them."

Storytelling is the age-old way humankind has used to make sense out of life. The Bible is a collection of these stories. The Jewish people (in order to gather strength in adversity, to hold them together when everything was going wrong, to celebrate a victory or to share their good feelings about being Jews) recited these stories, or read the poems, or chanted or danced to words or music that had a way of recalling the deeds that delivered them from the enemy. The scriptures were the stories of a people which were told or read whenever the community assembled. Power came to them as they heard these deeds retold. They entered into their history as it was recalled and they became a part of it. The imagery of Ezechial's dry bones is apt: "I will put sinews upon you to make flesh grow over you, cover you with skin and put spirit in you so that you may come to life. . . ." The bones rattle and they come together joint to joint.

Those who stood before a leader like Dr. Martin Luther King and heard him tell the history of black America or his dream for America could feel the tingle in one's bones and adrenalin flowing through their arteries as they felt themselves identified with a history or a movement in which all were becoming one. Their pain became transformed into creative energy. They experienced an inner freedom.

The recalling of the story is not new information of past events. Rather, it is a way of helping us to tap into the energy or spiritual power that is at work in history. It is this power, this dynamic, which will enable us to carry forward the past into the future. The story is like flowing water, carrying all who identify with it and even all of mankind—including those who denounce it.

Storytelling is a part of every family. At table or other family gatherings older members like to talk about their childhood, the eccentricities of their grandparents or other relatives and neighbors, the depression era, the war years, the moves because of neighborhood change or job transfers, the illnesses and deaths. Like the bible stories they are not scientific facts but simply the impressions that remain with us. Stories are told to children at bedtime not for information or learning but to give comfort and protection against the wild dreams that might terrify a child at night. Storytelling is not an idle pastime, for they convey the myths by which we live.

The shared stories of adults shape a history on which one can build a life of one's own apart from the family and be a source of strength as one reflects upon it in times of stress in later life. The stories that are articulated and celebrated form the springboard that helps us plunge into life. It gives one the bounce that helps a person plunge into the unknown. Without an identification with our history through words, song, or dance or some form of ritual we may stand at the side of a pool fixated at the water without the power to risk jumping in. We stand tall only when we stand on the shoulders of our forebears which comes from articulating our history or drawing together our history.

There are many ways of telling our story outside of a tribal ritual. The neighborhood tavern has always been a place for male society and the hairdressers a forum for women where ordinary people can spin the web of their lives with the people in these places who have the humanity and sensitivity to emphatically respond.

Many years ago I advocated a federation of

Catholic bartenders who see their vocations as gurus to comfort their clients who are in mourning. I have long maintained that we should give more recognition to the profession of bartending in the field of spiritual healing. When a person is confused, depressed, discouraged, or mixed up, there is a need to turn to someone. The troubled patron may not be able to go home and confront the grief situation at its source. It may never have occurred to this person to ring the rectory doorbell and ask the priest who is on call for spiritual healing. It may be that there is no priest in the rectory whom the parishioner would trust to be neutral, understanding and skilled in listening. Besides what "little person" wants to bother a priest and feel foolish and guilty talking about one's feelings. The atmosphere is more comfortable than a rectory parlor. A drink and a sympathetic bartender can draw a person out.

"The importance of listening," writes Arthur L. Foster, "is everywhere stressed in our culture—in business, in education, in psychotherapy, and in family relations, for example. Yet the experience of being really listened to is relatively rare; so rare in fact that people base friendships on this capacity alone, and pay considerable sums for the privilege of conversing with a professional who is educated in the art of listening. It is as if everyone recognizes intuitively his profound need to be heard; while at the same time relatively few persons possess the power to listen to another deeply enough or long enough to satisfy this human longing."

Listening is a gift to be celebrated and an art that all of us can improve. Marriages may falter, not because of poor housekeeping but because of poor listening. It may not be that partners are poor listeners or unconcerned people, but that they may not have allowed time for it. What is more comforting at the end of a day than a cup of tea with a loved one as we unravel the story of our day. Listening is the power that calls us out of ourselves. The alternative is the inescapable loneliness of being cut off from others and ultimately from ourselves. Listening to another's story tells the other he is worthwhile. It is an answer to a human cry for friendship.

I made a pastoral call on Mary Murphy, a patient in a psychiatric ward of a local hospital. This attractive Irish-born housewife told me that she felt very lonely in her basement apartment when her husband went off to work in the morning. It was so different from the old country where you were welcome in every one's home every hour of the day. The kettle was always on the stove and no one was too busy for a cup of tea. I fantasized that the only reason that she was on the "Fourth Floor" was that there was no one in her neighborhood to offer her a cup of tea. There was no one to celebrate her presence and listen to her story.

Self-analysis and introspection has limitations. It can be a circular or spinning motion that keeps us locked within ourselves as our lives whirl about in ever greater velocity but not moving away from the center of our anxiety. On the contrary as we sit and talk to another about the day or some phase of our life we find relief—like the blind and the lame our eyes become opened and we can walk with upright posture.

But why do people spend phenomenal sums weekly with clinical psychologists in order to have someone listen to them? A woman when asked that question simply said, "It is worth it. No one else will listen to me." There are profound reasons why people cannot tell or listen to stories. As much as we desire friendship and we are aware of the therapeutic effects of being listened to, we are inclined to defend ourselves against being seen for who we are. We are afraid of being discovered. We may watch the face of the other with fear and trembling as we tell our story. We stand before the other in nakedness, vulnerable to the other's judgment, memory, and power to use what we say in a destructive way now or in the future. Is there any question why deep friendships in and out of marriage are so rare and precious? The transfer of power from one to the other demands a trust and a faith which are counter to the style of our business, bureaucratic, and technical society.

While it may be difficult for the storyteller to give an uncensored version of the incident, it is equally difficult for the listener to accept the story without inwardly censoring and judging the storyteller. To be open to the other's values means that the listener is subject to self-examination of his own values. To listen to another can threaten my own meaning system. I may feel that it has taken me long enough to put life together that I cannot afford to have my meaning structures collapse again. I cannot allow myself to be surprised.

It is through the skillful and empathetic listening of another that we come to shape our story. Our individual story, like a nation's or a family's, is constructed around significant events. Certain crucial events which changed the direction of our lives become the pillars on which the superstructure of our lives take shape. At certain stages of our lives, particularly in periods of grief, we rearrange the events that are the foundation of our story. We find new meanings for old happenings and new connections of the present with the past. We are always making course corrections, but it is during a person's final illness or old age that the story is being re-drafted for the last time. When all the parts are together and the person has a sense of satisfaction with the new configuration, the person is ready to die. The story is no longer disconnected bits and pieces, good times and bad but one life seen through many prisms. Ministering to the dying person is largely facilitating this process. One's silent presence and an understanding heart is helping the person edit the final copy.

We are more concerned here with the use of storytelling as a way to handling normal grief than the completed copy at death. If grief has become sidetracked in withdrawal or acting out, the way back to the main road is sought by reconnecting the broken-off parts of our life through the device or articulating our feelings to another. This is what healing is about. It is finding meaning in our present loss through linking our present feelings with our history. It is another revision of our history. The present event becomes woven into the fabric of our story or to use an earlier metaphor, the foundation pillars or stones are rearranged to support the weight that has been added to the edifice.

Dr. Ira Progoff, a Jungian psychotherapist, offers a model for storytelling which is unique and into which one is initiated through a workshop. The workshop is neither a series of lectures nor therapy sessions. He is not dealing with pathologies but how healthy people move to a deeper level of inner awareness. The basic tool of the Intensive Journal Workshop is the workbook through which one catches the flow of one's own life.

The first exercise is to mark off a significant period in one's recent history and write about the important events surrounding it. In this period one can see on paper the highs and lows and possibly discern a pattern. The purpose is not analysis or interpretation but simply to put pieces together as we do with a jigsaw puzzle. It helps one catch the flow of life passing through our personhood in a way that helps us see life holistically. After we have identified the major events on which our life pivots, gradually one's life comes together and makes sense. We more and more affirm our history. It also offers us a way of going back to past events and re-living them. Indeed we can make contact with a deceased person and talk to them in the here and now as though the person were sitting in the empty chair across from us. We look into the same eyes we somehow could not look into before. History becomes present in this process, painful at times to the point of tears, but we learn to move through our tears and abdominal pains and come to an at-peaceness with this aspect of our past.

While our up-dated story defines us and gives us firm ground on which to stand, our greatest resource in the face of crisis is a guru friend, a significant person with whom we can relate day-by-day or week-by-week what is going on in the depths of our being. By listening to ourselves in the presence of another, what was below the level of our consciousness, stirring around in our dreams and fantasies now becomes articulated. We make the connections for ourselves. We need a friend to be with us as we enter the pain of events that were even ecstatic but now become fearful because they can never again be experienced. It is going down into the valley of darkness to link the broken cables and have new energy move through our lives. It is difficult to appreciate until after the fact that events we hide from ourselves become a source of strength when exposed.

In the process of going down into the pit we dig up the corpse which we hid but never buried. By telling the story of what we hid from ourselves, we are receiving forgiveness from ourselves and from those who are listening. More and more we see that forgiveness takes place in life more often than in the sacrament of reconciliation. The sacrament only celebrates the healing, the forgiveness, the coming together that has happened when one person was telling his story to another. Telling our story, particularly the dark side, what we had hid in our closet or backyard is a way of saying good-bye. The grieving comes to an end when the event has been redeemed. It now becomes a mark of victory, like the wounds of the risen Christ, or the cross changed from the stigma of infamy to a bejeweled ornament. It is a sharing of the Easter mystery, the Kingdom is at hand.

The person living in sorrow is well served by his compassionate friends, but heavy burdens are better borne by many hands. The active support of a caring community is a significant source of strength for one recovering from a loss. A caring community is one that takes the initiative, that reaches out to the ailing member and offers its healing powers. A staff member of the Paulist Center in Boston explains his understanding of a church community as a caring or therapeutic community. The caring or healing takes place simply by the hurting person joining and sharing the life of the community. This is contrasted with the concept of the parish church as a spiritual service center where the person contracts for specific services such as confession, communion, weddings or burials but not for membership with Christians who are trying to find meaning in the struggle of life simply by sharing their burdens and joys in a context that is larger than their family or neighborhood.

If a community is characterized by loving concern, it will emphasize the interaction of the members. Its opposite, the spiritual service station, offers its goods packeted for individual use and special occasions. The latter concentrates on a specific ritual service rather than the natural support of caring and sharing people of which ritual is a part. In the service station model the sacraments are dispensed to souls rather than seen as a way of ritualizing the pain of a life shared, lifted up and celebrated by the entire community. The caring community is not designed to take away the pain through spiritual prescriptions that anesthetize the hurt but rather to help the person enter the spiritual joy of union with God as one continues to live in sorrow.

A caring community must be small enough for its members to keep in touch with what is going on in each other's lives. Ideally this caring community would seem to be the family, the people who are sheltered by the same roof and serve each other at the family table. In reality this may not be our caring or support community. The family itself may be focused on the loss or the sorrow, such as—a death, an illness, a divorce or a serious conflict in values. We need extended families.

Our support system may be an interlocking of many systems. We may have one or two close friends at work who understand us not simply as workers but people who can be hurt and bleed when cut. It may be someone from the old neighborhood whose wisdom we still cherish or one or more relatives. We may never have realized that we had a support system or a caring community until a loss occurred. It is like our biological system. When one member of the body is damaged, the entire system rallies until equilibrium is restored.

In a long settled rural area we see how the community rallies at the death of a neighbor. On the physical level of preparing and serving food during the wake and after the funeral, the bereaved are tangibly affected by this caring. Sophisticated people can easily overlook the spiritual support that is given through serving a hot meal to the family in sorrow. To people close to the soil, words are not as precious as deeds. The offering of a hot dish to a family or person in sorrow can be a powerful expression of concern and support that can help people mobilize their inner forces again to face life.

The hurting person must send out signals that are loud and clear enough to be heard. Often hurting people deny their hurt with, "it is really nothing, it will all go away." The caring community at times must take the initiative to penetrate the facade and with great sensitivity question these non-responses to severe losses. Each person has a unique gift to offer another. The housewife can bake a cake. The grandfather can offer wisdom. A teen-ager can babysit. The parish priest can offer ritual or religious symbols congruent with the person's religious traditions. A support community has a diversity of gifts. But like all gifts of the Spirit, they are given for the benefit of the entire community. When, in the depths of grief, others share and care and understand, the tears, the anger, the guilt and the fear are all brought into perspective and down to manageable size. And this sharing is a two-way street. The grief of one member helps the community stay in touch with its own shared humanity, its own individual and collective need for their loving God.

CHAPTER SIX

Spiritual Healing

Grieving is saying goodbye. The reason for grieving is one's unwillingness or inability to let the past go. The past had its satisfaction, the beautiful memories and moments of the past make this understandable. Who wants to say goodbye to what has been precious, a beautiful relationship, a job that gave us an identity, a home that symbolized a life of love.

There are also satisfactions that are perverse and to which we cling to in all their ugliness. We wonder what satisfaction a dog gets from gnawing at a clean bone, wasting its energy in the biting, tugging, relentless war on a bone that seemingly has nothing to offer but futility. It is difficult to say goodbye to someone in whom we have invested a goodly portion of our lifetime even if hatred predominated.

It is the same reason nations make war rather than peace. We would rather be an enemy than a friend. We would rather hold a grudge than let it go. Perversity has its own satisfactions as destructive as it may be to our self and the other. It is our sinful condition, the unredeemed part of us, the little ball which we call the demonic, the will to destroy ourselves.

Grieving is calling out the Evil Spirit, the destructiveness in our lives. It is calling us from darkness to light. It is Jesus saying, "Come forth, leave this person. Let go of the relationship." The dark side of us, responds: "I am willing to leave, but the person would be in the state of collapse if I did. I am needed." Jesus, our true self, may say: "You know that this is a rationalization, not coming from the bowels of your personhood, your better self. You are deceiving yourself, not me. Let the tiny light of your true feelings and conscience emerge and gradually swallow up the darkness."

The resolution of our grieving begins when we hold out our hand in friendship and symbolically make peace with what has been taken from us. It is saying to that person, job, status, age bracket we have passed, "It is finished. It is time to separate and move on."

How is it that people delay grief or die without coming to terms with the loss? This is the mystery of iniquity. We must simply acknowledge that sinfulness is deeply rooted in our nature. It is not personal sin which we see and acknowledge for what it is, but the perverse side of the human condition from which we must be extricated by divine grace. Grieving is a way of communicating with God.

Grieving is the process of forgiving. It is saying that the past is accepted. It is all right. The rupture is healed. It is Abraham called to move on. It is letting go. It is a "leap" of faith. Jesus did not want to say goodbye from the cross. He struggled with it in the garden, complained about being deserted in his grieving by his three companions. He was able to say goodbye to his mother, but did not die without complaining to his father for having deserted him. Not until he entered this last protest did he finally accept it in its completeness as his head hung with the last gasp.

When we say that grieving is simply making peace with our past it sounds as easy as turning the pages of a history book. When we compare it to Jesus accepting the cross and dying with resignation, we may somnolently nod our heads as we do during the Sunday sermon. The healing process, on the contrary, is so extremely painful and visceral that we often prefer to float on the shallow waters of life or die an early death. It is only when one enters fully into the healing process that one understands the bloody sweat of the garden of Gethsemani. It is in this crucible of blood and guts we let the echo of his words reverberate within us: "Let this cup of suffering pass from me, but not my will but thine be done." After the garden, where resolution begins, there is the way of the cross and the crucifixion. Grieving is not simply achieved by thinking about the loss, however prayerfully we accept it. It must be finished by struggling with the memories that are daily evoked by persons, clothing, furniture, music, places, anniversaries and celebrative occasions. There is no rising with Jesus or spreading our wings again like an eagle as we feel a renewed youthful surge within us, unless we retrace our steps through what may have been a path of tears. There may be a dreadful wrenching of the spirit before we are at last free of the bondage of the past. When this new freedom comes, the scars of the past become the bejeweled cross of victory. It is pain transcended by being embraced, pain turned into joy by simply allowing it to be, without wallowing in it or being submerged by it.

The grief process is fittingly brought to a close with a celebration. In a farewell ceremony we pay tribute to the past as we move to the next stage of life. At a wedding, families eat, drink and make merry as they complete the grief of losing a son or daughter to the household and anticipate the joy of having a new family being born and the life of the clan perpetuated.

A celebration is letting go of the past in a way that it will not cripple or immobilize us. It is not blotting out the past so that it ceases to be a memory. The person who will never re-arrange the furniture of the room in which the deceased person slept and the person who quickly sells the house to blot out the memory of the stressful events are both in the same bind. It is the same phenomenon as the man or woman who can never return to their place of work or return to the neighborhood of their childhood. Just as one can become fixated in the past by the decor of a home, the pictures on the wall, or conversation about the old neighborhood, one can go to the other extreme and feverishly be occupied with the present and future so that there is no quiet moment of reflection that could lead back to the painful period that one cannot bear to re-live. A celebration is a way to facilitate this movement, but the timing must be right or ripe.

Amnesia or forgetfulness is a way to exile and remembrance is a way to forgiveness. The charasmatic movement has given us the beautiful expression "the healing of the memory." The healing of memories is not quite as miraculous or mysterious as it sounds. In pre-literate tribal life, highly literate ancient Greek society and the medieval town songs, plays, poetry, myths, and simply recounting past events were the ways people were able to tie their present life to the past so that they could find meaning for the future. Therapy and spiritual healing of memories were done through drama. People could act out or see acted out in a way they could identify the events that were blockages in their human development. They could dance with, scream at, or kill vicariously the people of their past whom they loved or hated. Our society seems to think that it has invented spiritual healing through psychotherapy and mysticism rather than having discovered new ways of doing what the ancients did well.

Each person has at particular junctions of life acute needs to tell their story in a community ritual. Since we do not have tribal dances, totems, Greek plays, or medieval liturgies, we must find substitutes that fit our culture, something more creative than pot parties for the young and drinking bouts for all ages. Our party rituals to have their therapeutic effects must help us to identify ourselves as members of a historical community in such a way that we find acceptance and meaning with it. In a highly individualistic world that lacks community ritual we must lean heavily on the professional therapists and social workers to prevent us from becoming alienated from ourselves. Parties that celebrate our histories can be powerful rituals to facilitate our grieving.

In the absence of parish, neighborhood and ethnic celebrations, we are thrown back upon our friends. Even married people have difficulty in telling their story to each other. In this country Marriage Encounter is spreading rapidly among church affiliated couples as a method of helping couples talk to each other about the present. It teaches them to talk about their history in a way that healing takes place and memories begin to reveal the loving presence of God in events that were too dreadful to look at alone.

To put all the burden of storytelling on marriage is unreal. It overloads the circuits. The nuclear family is limited in its healing powers. Each person needs a circle of friends with whom he or she can spin out the web of one's life and talk and walk with them down the trails of life and enter with friends the dark caverns of blocked out memories of joyful events that can never be celebrated again and times of stress that cause us to tighten up and scare us at the very mention of them. The valley of darkness is not simply the shortness of life and an approaching death but is peopled by the skeletons in our closet that haunt us in our dreams and dictate our neurotic behavior.

Sorrow or grief is everyman's way to God. It is so much a part of life that it hardly seems conceivable that one could come to the love of God without the struggles that come with significant losses in life. The sorrow may be experienced by the teen who breaks up with her boy friend, a rejection by a college board of admissions, a misunderstanding with one's parents that means packing up and shipping out. Whatever the loss and no matter how many times we come to this crisis situation, each time we must ask the profound questions about life: Who am I? What is life about? What road will I take as I come to this fork? How will I deal with the losses I fantasize by not taking the other road? When we are unglued, feeling helpless, we are open to an experience of God, called the dark night of the soul. We may cease to feel our loneliness as we enter the well and allow ourselves by sitting in silence to touch the wellsprings of divine life where all life is nourished at its Source.

Grief or sorrow is fertile soil for mystical experience. It is possible only when we experience our own nothingness as we wait in darkness for the light to penetrate our being. It does not necessarily take away our sorrow or sadness but transforms it into a source of energy, awareness of all of life's creativity. At a meeting of married couples talking about happiness in marriage, a woman said that the happiest moment of hers was when she and her husband stood at the graveside of their child as he was lowered into the grave. It sounds like a moment of mystical union, the still point, or however we describe touching God.

The unknown author of the now popular medieval book on prayer, *The Cloud of Unknowing* tells us that the way to union with God is letting go of the images of God so that we may be in contact with the Unknowable and be one with this Presence. We could enter the monastic state or make a thirty-day retreat to get in contact with God in this contemplative way, but a deep loss in our life can bring us to this type of prayer without the monastic trappings that are the luxury of religious, clergy, and Gov. Jerry Brown of California. It can bring us to a new level of prayer that does not use works of praise or an aggressive posture of petition, but to an attentive listening to the voice that issues from the depths of being.

When a person who has spent a life in developing and building a network of functions, skills, possessions, relationships, loves and loyalties, experiences a significant loss, something happens to his meaning system. The core of his life has been damaged.

Sorrow does not automatically offer meaning or the illumination of God's Presence. A colleague tells how a close friend called and related the tragic death of a child. Would he celebrate the funeral liturgy? He agreed but felt he would be too numb to have anything to say in a homily. He, like the parents, was stunned at this senseless act. How could he find God's activity in this action? It had no meaning for him. His faith in the power of ritual and community to pull himself and the mourners through the burial service was all he had to go on.

He sat at the wake with other mourners. As he talked with people and found that simply being in the presence of these caring people something was moving inside of him. No one was offering him meaning. It was simply being discovered by his participation in a loving community. The next morning as he led the community of worshipers in the liturgy, the movement toward meaning within him became more assertive. The community was drawing strength now, not simply from each other, but from the Christian symbols that had been their source of strength as they faced other crises in life. The symbols began to speak from the depths of the centuries of wisdom and solace which they offered to many cultures and people without number. His homily then became simply a part of the larger rituals in which this Catholic community had immersed themselves in this hour of grief. It was a lifting up of the belief that until now was dormant. The Catholic ritual helped pull this community of believers to some understanding of the place of the tragic in human life. It was a resource for the mourners who could identify with these symbols at this juncture of their journey. The dead bones of ritual pulsated with the life of the community.

Ritual is a part of the spiritual healing in the grieving process. A lighted candle, holy water, rosary, confession, daily Mass are ways people have to focus their inner life and find communion with God. Just because they may be used superstitiously by some, it in no way detracts from the power they had and have in people's lives. In the decade since Vatican II we have been like people cleaning house after a death: we have been too quick in throwing objects out which at a later date we may wish to cherish. The sanctuary light is a case in point. Zen is telling us of the importance of the candle to help us focus for prayer in depth.

The funeral rite is an obvious example. After the new funeral liturgy was established, I went as a mourner to the funeral of a Catholic with some Protestant friends. As we sat in the restaurant afterwards, they critiqued the service for me. With their pastoral counseling orientation they referred to the total service as "inspirational repression." Their main complaint was with the homily. The homilist talked about death abstractly and not about the deceased man who lived and died a tragic life. The celebrant did not help the family grieve or deal with their feelings, whatever they might be. A way of talking about a tragic death must be found simply because it is real and felt by the people in the pews.

My friends were saying that ignoring the man's life, no matter how mundane, and substituting religious thoughts on death and the Risen Christ, is repression. No matter how inspiring the service may be, these repressed feelings will demand that they

103

be dealt with at a later date. Repressed feelings fester and infect the entire system. The funeral ritual is one place to deal with grief.

We talked about Protestant funeral hymns that have gone the way of the Latin dirges. As maudlin as they were, they dealt with grief and loss. At many Catholic cemeteries we repress a healthy expression of grief by building chapels for the burial service. After the relatives are gone a work crew does the burying in assembly line fashion. The relatives cannot express their grief in the age-old healthy way of seeing their friend or relative lowered into the bosom of the earth while each mourner throws a symbolic spade of dirt upon the casket.

The resurrection theme can be a great aid to the grief process but not a short cut for it. It is not useful until the loss has been dealt with humanly. Inspirational repression is our method of not getting involved. It is a way of not taking the feelings of the other person seriously, lest we become ourselves emotionally involved. We do this with our friends when we try to cheer them up in moments of depression or tell them not to be worried when they are walking around with a hang-dog look. Our ideal model should not be Madison Avenue cool but rather Jesus of Nazareth who suffered every kind of human feelings—joy, love, grief and loss. The climax of his story began in the Garden of Olives and it is no accident that we call it the Passion. The path of Calvary was paved with fear, pain, anger and doubt. We cannot share in his glory until we too walk that path.

Our funerals should deal with both sides of the coin: the tearing asunder of relationships through death and the promise of an everlasting life of joy, peace, brotherhood and glory. In no way am I suggesting that we go back to the black vestments after we have had the white. From my experience as a pastor, the mass of the resurrection can be a healthy interlude in the grief process. By no means does it bring cloture to a significant loss, but a healthy relief from a grief that can be too burdensome and unproductive without this interlude. While I affirm the present ritual, I am pleading that within the context of hope, we keep alive the pain-joy tension through our choice of words, music, and our celebrative posture.

Grieving is best seen as a long-term process like personality change or spiritual growth. There may be an identifiable moment when it all comes together but enduring healing is effected by a sustained effort to lead the new life. To have a guru-friend, someone to help us put our story together is the largest piece of the puzzle which when all the pieces are in place gives meaning to life. A supportive community is another large piece. If the grieving person comes from a culture that has strong familial bonds there is a built-in support system. Everybody rallies to comfort the person in distress.

In some cultures there is a detailed ritual for the bereaved that reminds the community of their duty to them. The armbands on the sleeves of the males and the black dress worn by the bereaved women and bunting on public buildings are relics of societies that knew something instinctively about the community aspects of grief. With the advent of the nuclear family, the family or clan is less supportive to members experiencing serious losses. We grieve over neighborhood change, divorces, failing college entrance exams, and scores of sophisticated types of losses but have not developed rituals which the community can use to support its mourning members. Since our expectations of a "happy", pain-free life have escalated, and we have not designed adequate grieving rituals, then we must face frustration, loneliness, and isolation in a way that no society has yet experienced. This helps us understand crime and violence in America.

While our society has not ritualized grief adequately, it has formed enormous types of support groups to meet highly specialized needs. There are Parents Without Partners, parents who are child beaters, parents of retarded or handicapped children, Alcoholics Anonymous, prayer groups and groupings of senior citizens without number. In any large urban area there is the possibility of finding a group to share each of these unusual human concerns which can be especially supportive while a person is going through a crisis of grief. The least group members can do for the grieving person is not to permit him to withdraw completely, to encourage him to keep up his active membership in society. Such groups need not be professional therapy sessions for grieving people. They function simply by offering support and structure to those who would otherwise weep alone. In the final analysis, healing is the experience—at a profound level—that one is not alone, that one can tap reserve sources of strength, that one does not have to be anything other than one's true self. To be healed is to see the glimmer of light at the far end of the tunnel. Then it doesn't matter that there is still a long way to walk!

CHAPTER SEVEN

The Call to a New Beginning

How long does one grieve? How long is the mourning period? We grieve until we are finished, until we can put the experience of loss behind us and find new meaning and hope in our present and future. Grieving is being involved in a process of nature which has its own dynamic. All of life has a rhythm. We cannot ruthlessly impose our reason upon it without in some way maiming that life. Like a current of water gushing down a mountain or the energies of a child, we can help channel or divert the flow of power and life but we must respect the inner nature of this source of energy and its need to run its course according to its own pace. Good grieving, then, is the process of helping the sorrowing person to get in touch with that inner flow of life with all its pain as the person experiences this significant loss.

When we are cut off from a partner, job, status, a limb that was an integral part of life, the entire inner person needs to withdraw. One feels cut off from a major source of life. There may be nd we wander in the desert even though the externals of life seem unchanged. Briefly, we have been separated from a vital part of us. We are out of contact with an inner source that nourished our very being. How does this process reverse itself so we can begin to affirm life again. This reversal of the flow of life cannot be manipulated through modern psychological techniques. We can facilitate it only by getting in contact with the organic flow of life that mankind was in touch with before the scientific and technological era.

Our Judaic-Christian heritage offers us some understanding of the lost art of grieving and restoration to a hope-filled life. Our Christian heritage stems originally from the Jewish tradition which is a feeling religion. But after a few centuries of Christianity the influence of the Greek ideal of a rational or intellectual approach to life predominated over the earlier, more earthy approach.

What we *think* about our grief is not to be equated with grieving. Studying or thinking about grief is not grieving. Intellectualizing about grief is 180 degrees from being in the process of grieving. Nevertheless we can look to the Bible, particularly the Old Testament to find models for meaning and see the actuality of God's people working through personal and social grief. The Jews were not gentle people when they were engaged in anger and were wrestling with God for forgiveness or demanding to be delivered from captivity or whatever. They were able to stand God to the teeth in crisis because they knew he loved them and would deliver on his promise to be their God.

The book of Job is an excellent source for a person who is ready to move from grief to accepting and affirming the reality of one's present life. Job is brought face to face again and again with the mystery of a God of justice who makes the good man suffer. Through a dialogue with three friends he confronts the notion that his suffering is a punishment for his personal sins. We, today, find ourselves in the company of the same three. Their names are Self-doubt, Poor self-image, and Readiness to beat ourselves while we are doing the best we can.

Job did not accept this heavy trip his friends were laying on him. Although he did not understand why he was tortured in soul and body, he refused to accept the guilt his friends were putting on him. Nor did he blame God. What carried Job through these crises was his faith in God as one who cares about him. Yet Job wanted to give a human answer to his misery, but Yahweh cut him short. Since man cannot fathom the depths of God's wisdom, he cannot have a completely satisfying answer. It is faith or trust that compensates for the enigma of senseless suffering and futile grief.

In the bitter struggles of life, evil and suffering seem often to be the winners. Faith does not simply step in and tip the balance in favor of sweet goodness. Nor does faith clinch the eternal philosophical arguments over evil. What faith accomplishes is better understood in terms of insight into a larger reality. Faith removes the blinders so we can choose a meaningful goal. In faith we are freed from the vicious circles which drain us and waste our precious energies. In our times we are beginning to look more benignly at faith healing. It is not seen as magic or witchcraft but a belief that life is a process in which God is present in the hopeless, cruel, and destructive situation to those who believe. They believe that this approach to God not only gives them peace of mind but leads to and indeed accomplishes outstanding examples of people being healed physically as well as spiritually. Through faith, people "take up their bed and walk." People in the helping professions can testify to the healing power of people of faith.

The healing of the body through faith is associated with the healing of memories. It is easy to understand how healing takes place when we re-live the hurts of the past, come to some new understandings of our childhood, forgive our deceased parents for offenses they never imagined, and above all forgive ourselves and accept our history. Through this process, which we described under the rubric of storytelling we can better understand what charis-

111

matics refer to as the healing of memories. Our life becomes integrated, not only our past, present and future, but our mind and body come together, the spiritual and physical relate harmoniously. Skin diseases, nervous tics and other ailments disappear as the memories are healed, they claim.

It is easy to talk about faith as though it were a commodity, a garment, or even a neat set of doctrines rather than an emergence to a new level of humanity, new life, or an inner light emerging from the struggle with darkness. Scripturally orientated faith is not a head trip. This anthropomorphic expression of faith lets God know how wretched we feel in this hour of his abandonment of us. When contrasted with polite society's sweet words, soft music, and unwillingness to confront God about the chaotic situation we are in, it is an earthy way of struggling with our feelings about ourselves, life, and even the seemingly calloused way God at times treats his friends. The psalms exemplify the way we turn from grief to hope, neither of which are bland, sweet nothings.

Lord, don't be angry and rebuke me!
    Don't punish me in your anger!
Have pity on me, because I am worn out;
    Restore me, because I am completely
        exhausted;
        my whole being is deeply troubled.
How long, Lord, will this last?

Come and save me, Lord;
    because you love me, rescue me from
    death.
In the world of the dead you are not
    remembered;
    no one can praise you there!

I am worn out with grief;
    every night my bed is damp from my crying
    my pillow is soaked with tears.
My eyes are swollen from so much weeping,
    and I can hardly see—
    all because of my enemies!

The Lord hears my weeping;
    he listens to my cries for help,
    and answers my prayers.

Psalm 6

At a recent adaptation of the Seder supper we dipped bitter herbs into the haroses (horseradish) and then I read: "Our fathers were able to withstand the bitterness of slavery because it was sweetened with the hope of freedom? By sharing in the bitterness of Christ's sufferings we strengthened our hope." Then the Pauline reading: "We exult in tribulations also, knowing that tribulations work out endurance and endurance tried virtue and tried virtue hope. And hope does not disappoint because the charity of God is poured forth in our hearts by the Holy Spirit who has been given to us."

113

When these readings and ritual are shared in some form of community of loving people the bitterness of life has a sweet savor and grieving turns to joyful acceptance of life and renewed energies to face life again. The faith of the community is stronger than the sum of the faith of the individuals, a deep source of strength, support and meaning.

Shared faith in a community context nourishes and deepens this faith and becomes operative when we come to grief. While we subscribe to our belief that faith is a gift of God, we are also aware that faith is like a seedling that needs to be nourished. The person who is always on the cutting edge of life, taking risks and trusting life is living out his faith in action. It is the faith that tells us that Christ did not die between two candle sticks but between two thieves and trusted in his Father not to desert him in his agony and death. It is a faith that we see in the weatherbeaten faces of people who have endured life and are quite content to live or die.

Robert Coles, commenting on the biographies of *Social Security Beneficiaries Who Reached the Age of 100,* tells us how facing life itself generates faith: "Many of the people who appear have a rock-bottom religious faith that will not be deterred. Yet, some are not formally religious, simply old and wise and again resigned to nature's if not God's ways. Accordingly, they don't come up with dogmatic explanations for their longevity, nor do they want to prescribe all sorts of advice for theirs, or lecture the young on their waywardness—with the implication that theirs will not be long life because of this or that. True, many worked hard, lived moderately, prayed earnestly—and are more than willing to attribute their continued existence to such habits of mind and body. Yet, again, the majority of these men and women are shrewd and humble enough to bow before fate and say a simple thank you (rather than moralize); or to say that they don't quite know how they did it, how it happened—but they come from long-lived families, and perhaps that is that."

We have described the process of moving from a state of mourning to an affirmation of life. The religious man gains from his faith the energy and motive to turn back into life with renewed spirit. Simple endurance tides people over the continuous new twists and turns in life. No matter what the specific circumstances, the process is similar in structure for most. The person initially feels cut off from a nourishing source of life. Then there is the period of inner healing and integration, acceptance of the fact, even if there is no outward movement. The next stage often happens in silence or a reflective moment. It might be a child running, a new shoot on a plant, a song, a bird singing, a touch, or a word. More than likely it will happen while we are unaware of it, as in sleep. Contact is again made with all of reality. Life comes together again. We begin to reach out to find new interests, new friends, new ways of relating. The Easter mystery is made present.

With our friends who are grieving we must realize that it is not our life but theirs. It is not for us to tell people how to grieve but we can be sensitively present to them and offer our assistance. At the right moment we might invite the widow to a party of married couples and let her struggle through this experience. We might ask the newly divorced man or woman how it feels and give them the invitation to feel free to talk about the new status. We might call on our retired boss or invite him back to an office party. Grief work is a community effort. We try to make it easy for the grieving person to return and start another chapter of one's life. We know when the grieving is finished. Joy has returned like the swallows to Capistrano. Energy abounds. Life is good. The sky is blue. God is alive and well. We feel his presence.

In ordinary conversation, faith and hope are interchangeable. Hope is a belief that life has a future. It is a conviction without evidence that the present no matter how destructive has promise. It is a belief that this activity, springing from the love of God in us, will endure forever. In some sense all our pain, all our grief, all our sorrow will be "eternalized." Somehow, it will remain, and cannot be destroyed by death. It is this hope that is the basis for the inner joy one sees on the face of people who have emerged from the tunnel, who have been to the well, or have come from the valley.

In *The Divine Milieu* (Harper & Row), Teilhard de Chardin talks about hope in human images: "A thought, a material improvement, a harmony, a particular expression of love, the enchanting complexity of a smile or a look, all the new beauties that appear for the first time, in me or around me, on the human face of the earth—I cherish them like children and cannot believe that they will die entirely in the flesh. If I believed that these things were to wither away forever should I have given them life?"

When each of us can put our struggles with life into this context of faith and hope, we can sing, dance and make love again with abandon. The power of Christ in the Christian symbols is the alchemy that changes the tragic into ecstatic joy.